I'LL BE THERE

(AND LET'S MAKE FRIENDSHIP BRACELETS)

A Girl's Guide
to Making and Keeping
Real-Life Friendships

AMY WEATHERLY AND JESS JOHNSTON

WITH WHITNEY BAK

Illustrated by Tequitia Andrews and Ashley Dugan

Tommy NELSON®

An Imprint of Thomas Nelson

I'll Be There (And Let's Make Friendship Bracelets)

© 2022 Amy Weatherly and Jessica Johnston

Tommy Nelson, PO Box 141000, Nashville, TN 37214

Published in Nashville, Tennessee, by Tommy Nelson. Tommy Nelson is an imprint of Thomas Nelson. Thomas Nelson is a registered trademark of HarperCollins Christian Publishing, Inc.

The authors are represented by Alive Literary Agency, www.aliveliterary.com.

Tommy Nelson titles may be purchased in bulk for educational, business, fund-raising, or sales promotional use. For information, please email SpecialMarkets@ ThomasNelson.com.

ISBN 978-1-4002-4178-1 (audiobook)
ISBN 978-1-4002-4176-7 (eBook)
ISBN 978-1-4002-4177-4 (SC)

Library of Congress Cataloging-in-Publication Data

Names: Weatherly, Amy, 1983- author.
Title: I'll be there (and let's make friendship bracelets) : a girl's guide to making and keeping real-life friendships / Amy Weatherly and Jess Johnston ; with Whitney Bak ; illustrated by Tequitia Andrews and Ashley Dugan.
Description: Nashville, Tennessee : Thomas Nelson, [2022] | Includes bibliographical references. | Audience: Ages 8-12 | Summary: "Friendships between tween girls are anything but simple. Sister, I am with you creators Amy Weatherly and Jess Johnston are here to help in this interactive girl's guide to making healthy and authentic friendships"— Provided by publisher.
Identifiers: LCCN 2022032460 (print) | LCCN 2022032461 (ebook) | ISBN 9781400241774 (paperback) | ISBN 9781400241767 (eBook) | ISBN 9781400241781 (audiobook)
Subjects: LCSH: Friendship—Juvenile literature. | Friendship bracelets—Juvenile literature.
Classification: LCC BF575.F66 W42 2022 (print) | LCC BF575.F66 (ebook) | DDC 158.2/5—dc23/eng/20220729
LC record available at https://lccn.loc.gov/2022032460
LC ebook record available at https://lccn.loc.gov/2022032461

Written by Amy Weatherly and Jess Johnston with Whitney Bak

Cover illustration by Tequitia Andrews/Lilla Rogers Studio

Illustrated by Tequitia Andrews and Ashley Dugan

Sticky note doodle © Shutterstock/Nikolaeva; abstract hand-drawn doodles © Shutterstock/mhatzapa; seamless pattern and hand-drawn doodles © Shutterstock/blue67design

Printed in the USA

22 23 24 25 26 LSC 6 5 4 3 2 1

Mfr: LSC / Crawfordsville, IN / October 2022 / PO #12144749

To our daughters, Oaklee, Haven, and Macall.

—Amy and Jess

For Pepper, Nova, and Happy. Thanks
for making me a mom and bringing
more joy than I ever dreamed of.

—Ashley

For my husband and children.

—Tequitia

Contents

A Letter to the Grown-Up

Hi!

We're Amy and Jess.

We're the writers behind the online community of over a million women called *Sister, I Am with You* that's dedicated to all things friendship. But even though our blog and our nationally bestselling book, *I'll Be There (But I'll Be Wearing Sweatpants)*, are written with adults in mind (because friendship is still hard and awkward as a grown-up, are we right?), the message is really for *every* age. Our own deep desire for friendship and connection started as young as preschool, but we never felt it more than we did in our elementary and tween years.

And so, we wanted to create a book specifically for young readers. We wanted to offer the book we needed when we were that age: the road map to authentic friendship. It's kind of like we wrote it for our younger selves—and we did write it for our own daughters, who are already maneuvering the tricky world of sisterhood.

It's written in a way so that your daughter can read this book all on her own. Or you can read it together. But either way, we hope that you have conversations about some of the important topics we tackle.

In addition to showing young girls how to make and keep true friendships, this book offers some of our most relatable stories, places to reflect and journal, interesting facts, fun quizzes, word searches, real-life challenges, hidden messages, and more! We're so excited for your daughter to dive into this interactive friendship guide.

Our heart behind this book is simple: We want young girls to know they are not alone. And though friendship can be hard and complicated, it's also so very worth it. So let's start this journey, and let's take it together.

Love,
Amy and Jess

1
When you Really need a Friend
(yeah, us too)

O h hey, we're Jess and Amy. And even though we met only a few years ago, we quickly became BFFs.

At first, we messaged each other all the time. We started with things like "Girl, those earrings look so cute on you." And "Have you ever had a Chick-fil-A sandwich with cheese on it? Because it's life changing, FYI." After a month or so we started chatting on the phone. That's when our friendship moved from talking about goofy, random things to sharing secrets and asking for advice.

We'd talk about everything. But we'd often come back to the topic of friendship.

We agreed that friendship was, and always has been, something we wanted. Like, *a lot*.

We talked about how hard it had sometimes been to make friends. How we had both moved and been the "new girl." How we were so happy when we finally found great friends, and how upsetting it was to be left out by girls at school. And we shared how we'd both been hurt by girls we thought would always be our friends but were only in our lives for a little while.

One day Amy called and said, "Jess, it happened again. I was the only one who didn't get invited to the party. I'm sitting alone in my closet crying. Why does this happen? Why does it hurt so much? What's wrong with me? Why don't people like me? I really hate this feeling."

Another day Jess said, "Amy, I don't belong. I still feel like the new girl sometimes. It seems like the people around me don't like who I am. It makes me feel so sad."

And yet another day Amy announced, "Jess, one of my best friends is moving away. I don't know what I'm going to do without her. I don't know how to make another friend as special as she is."

Over time, we shared all of this and more. And it felt wonderful to talk about things that really seemed to matter. We started to wonder why we didn't hear other girls doing the same. After all, we weren't the only ones who felt like this. Right?

So we started sharing about our friendship online, and, well, now it's kind of a thing. We write on our blog, *Sister, I Am with You*, share posts on social media, and talk to women about the topic of friendship—the ins and outs. The good and bad. The things we messed up, the things we got right, and the things we're still learning.

We have struggled with friendships at every age and every stage. And we often talk about all the things we wish someone had told us when we were younger. That's why we wrote this book just for **you**. It's filled with stories and advice and encouragement we could have used at your age (and we still need even as grown-ups).

So let's do this. Let's talk about friendship. And not just the kind of friendship where you dress in your cutest clothes and go somewhere special. Sure, that can be fun sometimes. But we want to talk about the kind of friendship that gets real. We're talking about

- the kind of friendship that's safe for big feelings, deep secrets, and laughing so hard you snort;
- the kind of friendship that understands you have homework and chores;

- the kind of friendship that makes bad days better;
- the kind of friendship that doesn't notice how expensive or trendy your clothes are—or aren't;
- the kind of friendship that's there for trips to the bathroom and sweaty laps around the gym;
- the kind of friendship that doesn't care what you eat for lunch or how many likes you get on TikTok—or even if you have a TikTok account; and
- the kind of friendship where you can say, "Hey, something is hanging out of your nose."

We're talking about friends who won't judge you—ever. Friends who won't care if you're more into playing sports or Minecraft or piano. Friends who want to hang out whether you're watching YouTube or jumping on a trampoline or painting your nails.

We're talking about belonging to each other—like really, really belonging. This is the kind of friendship that doesn't have to look cool or fit in with any kind of crowd. A friendship where you **can** curl up close in your sleeping bags and share your most embarrassing stories—no filters needed.

That's the kind of friendship we want. But sometimes we're stuck wondering, *Where do we even find friends like that?*

DID YOU KNOW?

Humans aren't the only living creatures that can make friends. Science proves that some of the smartest animals have friends too!

CHIMPANZEES
HORSES
HYENAS
ELEPHANTS
BATS
DOLPHINS
WHALES

Why does this matter? Because having friends helps these animals survive in the wild. And we need close friends to help us make it through life too. After all, it's a jungle out there![1]

Whatever your friendships have been like, we get it.

For example, have you ever walked into a birthday party and felt like no one wanted you there? Have you ever wanted to disappear, sneak away, or hide out near the snack table until it was time to leave? We have.

Have you ever walked away from meeting someone new and felt embarrassed and awkward, like you said all the wrong things? Yup. Us too.

Do you ever feel like you're not enough, like you are too shy, too boring, too awkward, or too average? Uh-huh, we've been there. And then we've spent the next day thinking of all the things we should have said. Maybe you're like us— we're very good at having conversations in our heads but not always great at having them in real life.

Also, PS: Disney movies really led us to believe that we were going to have perfect hair and beautiful singing voices and that everyone who would meet us would like us. We keep waiting to be magically transformed into a Disney princess, but nope, it still hasn't happened.

If you've ever learned on Monday that all your friends had a sleepover last weekend and you weren't invited— again, yup, we know that feeling. We feel sick just thinking about it.

If you've ever had a big fight with a friend and didn't know how to fix it, *ouch*, we've been there a time or two. Losing a friend hurts, and it makes you question yourself. Sometimes you stop trusting others, and you put up walls around your heart so that no one else can get close to you.

We understand how you feel. When we think of some

friendships we've lost, our hearts ache like the breakup was just yesterday.

If you've ever felt like you were too energetic or talked too much, us too. Doesn't everyone have days where they act like a golden retriever puppy that didn't get her fetch time? *I'm over here! Throw it this way! I just want to hang out with you!* No? Okay. Us either.

If you've ever said something so weird you wished your parents would transfer you to a new school—or, better yet, move to a new town—we get it. We've been there too.

If you've ever felt so busy with school and sports and music lessons and family and chores that it seems like you don't even have time for friendships, um, yes.

If you've ever had someone introduce herself to you even though you've met her ten times before, we are your people.

We've been there too.

"Hi. I'm _____. I don't think we've met."

We actually have met. We were in the same classroom last year. It's so nice to know I'm forgettable. Doesn't hurt at all.

We know the sting of being invisible. The feeling of being picked last for dodgeball or not having someone to partner with in science class. It makes us want to go home and cry too.

THIS IS YOUR SPACE TO
BE CREATIVE! COLOR,
JOURNAL, AND DOODLE
ALL YOUR THOUGHTS.

WRITE IT DOWN!

When you think about trying to make new friends,
how do you feel? Excited? Anxious? Nervous? Why do
you feel that way?

_____

_____

_____

_____

_____

_____

_____

Reread the bulleted list on pages 3-4 about the kind of friendship we're going to discuss in this book. What kind of friendship are you looking for?

_____

_____

_____

_____

_____

THE GOOD NEWS IS, YOU CAN TOTALLY HAVE A FRIEND LIKE THAT! IN THIS BOOK, WE'LL TELL YOU HOW.

STICKY NOTE CHALLENGE

Grab a sticky note and write these words: "I know my good friends are out there." Then, put it on your bathroom mirror where you can see it every day.

What if you don't know where to look for the better kind of friendship? What if you're even a little afraid to try? If that's you, we get it. You want to find friends who will laugh at your dumbest jokes. Friends who will help you learn new TikTok dances and share their favorite Takis. Friends who will understand if you say, "Honestly, I don't want to leave the house today. Wanna come over and make friendship bracelets?"

But what if you open up to people and they laugh at you? What if they reject you?

Your heart is your most sacred possession.

We've been there, and it's terrifying. Your heart is your most sacred possession. It can be scary to put yourself out there if it means someone might see the real you and walk away. And so, it's important to guard our hearts.

A Good Friend Is ...

Find and circle all the words hidden in the grid below.
Remember to look in every direction!

KIND   THOUGHTFUL   POSITIVE

HONEST   UNDERSTANDING   CARING

FUN   TRUSTWORTHY   APPROACHABLE

```
Y C A R I N G Z A R H C E F V
T R U S T W O R T H Y J G K V
H W R I Y N L Q N F Z V B R I
L G U N D E R S T A N D I N G
V I A B H V Y S A P Z I A T O
P P S U T A X S L P V F H Z F
F Q H U H N M C S R V H C L S
D P I Y O R K B B O E O L Y D
J O C E U F U B A A W N V D V
J S N G G Z U U S C Q E T K U
D I Z T H W J N M H Z S V A X
S T C Y T K V K Q A L T E N O
H I R H F Q I B K B L B S G D
L V M P U B J N W L P J A Q E
Q E R F L H V T D E G A C T L
```

On the other hand, what if you put yourself out there and discover the best friend you've ever had? What if the hard work of making a new friend is *so worth it* because that person will become a true friend who will always be there for you?

Notes for Your Grown-Up

If you want to share your friendship journey with your grown-up, write some notes from this chapter here.

_____

_____

_____

_____

As we get started, keep in mind that **this** book isn't a how-to guide to impress people so they'll be your friends. It's about finding people you like to spend time with who also like spending time with you.

It's about learning what makes a good friend and recognizing what doesn't.

It's about journeying through life with a bunch of awesome girls by your side—or even just one or two.

It's about weaving the threads of your story with theirs to create something that's unique and colorful and creative and beautiful, like the very best friendship bracelets. Something that's made to last and only gets stronger with each thread you add.

It's about being loved as we are, where we are, with what we have. Everyone should have friendships like that. Everyone *needs* friendships like that. And if you don't have those friendships, that's okay. Let's talk about it. Let's be honest about how this whole friendship thing is going. And then, let's find a way to make it better, together.

Get ready. Here we go.

Did you find the secret message?

Write it out here:

___ ___ ___   ___ ___ ___   ___ ___   ___ ___ ___!

2
When you're Lonely

I had the same best friend all throughout elementary school. It was awesome. We were always in the same class, and we always did everything together. We sat next to each other at lunch. We had sleepovers on weekends. We had matching outfits. Sometimes, her family even asked me to go on vacation with them.

But then, in the middle of our fifth-grade year, her friend from church moved to our school. Suddenly, it wasn't just the two of us anymore, and I felt so left out. I couldn't keep up with most of their conversations because they were about people and places I didn't know anything about. I thought I was being replaced and forgotten and rejected, and I couldn't help but feel a tiny bit jealous.

I know now that I probably could have handled things

differently and that there is usually room at the table for everyone. But back then, I missed my best friend, and I didn't know how to tell her.

This was just one of many times I learned that friendships are hard. But let me promise you this: Just because something is hard doesn't mean it can't be wonderful. Just because it was bad in the past doesn't mean it can't lead to something good.

> *Just because something is* *hard doesn't* *mean it can't be wonderful.* *

When we were younger, things seemed simpler. Back in kindergarten, we could walk up to **someone** and say, "Wanna be my friend?" It was that easy. And maybe you've made a few good friends this way. But as we get older, that doesn't really work anymore. We start to realize that friendship is messy—certainly not as simple as handpicking friends at random.

It's difficult when you and your friend are put in different classes. It's tricky when you have to choose between hanging out with someone who never wants to do things you enjoy and being bored at home. It's messy when someone you used to make jokes with becomes someone you avoid in the hallway. It's sad when someone you relied on like a sister becomes someone you can't trust to keep your secrets.

It's lonely.

It's lonely when you walk into the lunchroom and none of your friends are there or when the soccer season ends and you don't get to see your friends anymore during practice. And it's lonely when you don't even have a friend to lose in the first place.

It's lonely when your parents are fighting and you don't know who to talk to or when you read a **great** book and there's no one to share it with.

You're not alone in your loneliness. I've felt lonely too. It's quite possibly my least favorite emotion. But even if you feel that way now, you don't have to keep being lonely. You *can* make new friends.

I want people to feel less lonely. When people know they aren't alone, magic happens. They grow stronger, and they grow braver. They build make-believe worlds and create new inventions. They reach out and help others. They jump for joy. And I am here for it.

You're not alone in your loneliness.

Here's some good news: making new friends isn't actually that complicated. But it does take effort.

You'll have to show up when you want to stay home.

HAVE PEOPLE YOU TRUST

MAKE HEALTHIER CHOICES

Feel HAPPIER ☺

WHEN YOU AREN'T LONELY, YOU...

EXERCISE MORE

SLEEP BETTER

ARE LESS STRESSED

A+
DO BETTER IN SCHOOL

ARE LESS ANXIOUS

HAVE BETTER CONVERSATIONS'

You'll have to invite someone to hang out instead of waiting for them to invite you first. You'll have to jump on video calls, respond to chat messages, stand up for them when other kids are being jerks, and remember birthdays. You'll have to do the things your friends want—even when you'd rather do something else.

I'm often surprised at the girls who raise their hands and say, "Yeah, sometimes I get lonely." I think, *What? You're so nice. You seem like you'd have lots of friends! But you're telling me that deep down you feel lonely too? Hmm . . . seems suspicious, but okay.*

That's the thing about loneliness. Anyone can feel it.

It doesn't matter if you've got a big following or you're the lead in the school play. It doesn't matter if you live in a giant house or an apartment or an igloo. It doesn't matter if your nose **is** always stuck in a book or if you're always the first person picked for kickball games. Loneliness can strike anyone at any time.

If you're feeling lonely even though you have loads of friends . . . just know that it happens to all of us, and it's okay. Sometimes it means we're just feeling funky and we need a day or two to figure things out. Sometimes it means we need to appreciate the people right in front of our faces a little more. And sometimes it means we need

BE HONEST

When was the last time you felt lonely?

_____

_____

_____

_____

_____

How long did the loneliness last?

_____

_____

_____

_____

Did you do anything about it? Why or why not?

I'M SO SORRY YOU FELT THAT WAY. I'VE BEEN THERE TOO. BUT I WANT YOU TO KNOW THIS: YOU DON'T HAVE TO BE LONELY. NEXT TIME, YOU CAN CHANGE THINGS SO YOU WON'T BE ALONE. KEEP READING TO LEARN HOW!

21

to step back and ask ourselves if it's time to branch out and find some new friends.

If you decide the solution is to branch out, don't be afraid to stand up for yourself. If you're sitting at a lunch table with girls who don't cheer you on, encourage you, or want what's best for you, move to a different table. If those in your group ignore you, don't listen when you're trying to share something, or constantly put you down, maybe it's time to find a new group. Keep in mind, all friends will sometimes mess up. All friends will say hurtful things and accidentally interrupt. The key is to determine whether you usually feel confident and good about yourself when you're around them or if you tend to feel insecure and negative about yourself when you're with them. If they are critical of you or others, create drama, or aren't honest with you, they are not your people.

Of course, you don't have to throw your chair back from the table or make a scene. Just walk away calmly. Life isn't fun when you spend it in the wrong place with the wrong people. So learn to speak up. Say what you need to say and share how you feel in a kind and respectful way and move on. Then look for the people who are alone and build something new with them. People can't love someone they don't know, so make yourself known.

If you're feeling lonely because you're actually alone . . . please know you have the power to make a friend.

My friend Tori asked me to come over one day to eat lunch and watch *Toy Story 3*. (This might be a hot take, but TS3 is better than *Toy Story* or *Toy Story 2* or *Toy Story 4*. I said what I said.)

Tori and I watched the movie while we ate ham sandwiches and shared a bag of chips. It was perfect.

The thing is, Tori and I had never been close. We'd been friendly, but we usually hung out with different people. So I was surprised—and also super happy—when she invited me over.

Before I went home, I asked her what had made her reach out to me. I'll never forget her answer. She said, "I've been feeling lonely and sorry for myself for a long time. Finally I decided to do something about it. So I took a chance, and I thought of you. I realized the solution was inside of me all along."

I'm so glad she was brave enough to do that. And it taught me an important lesson: if you put yourself out there and invite someone to hang out, you could end up with a new best friend.

Maybe making friends now isn't so different from when we were in kindergarten after all.

STICKY NOTE CHALLENGE

Grab a sticky note and write down a compliment to a girl you could become friends with. You might write something like "I really like your hair today" or "Your presentation was so good!" Then, when the time is right, hand it to her in class. It's a great way to break the ice and help you move out of a season of loneliness.

If you're feeling lonely because you believe something is wrong with you . . . please keep reading. We'll talk about this later because it deserves its own chapter (see chapter 4), but for now, hear me say this: I promise, there is nothing messed up about you. Soon, you will find the friends who are just right for you.

If you're feeling lonely because you've gotten your feelings hurt before . . . I'm sorry. I'm sorry someone hurt you. I'm sorry you were betrayed. I know I can't do anything to erase what you've been through. But *please* don't let one bad friendship ruin you for good. There are, what, like four billion girls on this planet?

They're not all mean. They don't all gossip. They're not all just **waiting to** bring everyone else down.

Most want the same things you want. They want a real friendship. They want to let loose and have fun. They want to laugh. They want to hug. They want to cry. They want to share their deepest secrets. They want to feel seen and be known.

They won't **be** perfect. Perfect people don't exist—but awesome ones do. They're out there. I know it's hard to take a risk and raise **your** hand and admit that you get lonely. But my guess is that when you do, you'll find out you aren't so alone after all.

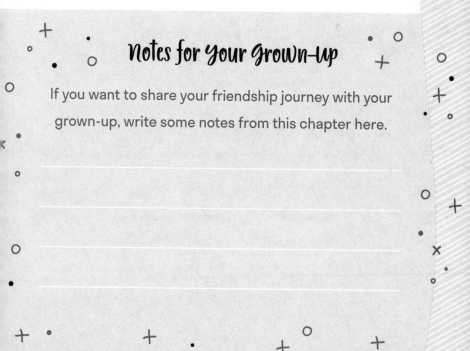

Notes for your Grown-up

If you want to share your friendship journey with your grown-up, write some notes from this chapter here.

Five Ways to Make New Friends

1. **Join a new activity.** Whether it's soccer or drama club or basketball or swimming or dance or an after-school art class, you'll meet people who like to do the same thing you do. That's a great way to start a friendship.

2. **Introduce yourself to someone new at school.** It doesn't matter if she just transferred to your school or if you've never had class together before or if she's someone you've seen around for years but you haven't taken the time to talk to. You might be surprised by how well you get along!

3. **Invite your neighbors to hang out.** Ask them to bike around the block with you, jump on a trampoline, or do anything else outside for an afternoon.

4. **Talk to other girls.** Strike up a conversation when you're at the park with your family, when you're at the lunch table at school, or when you're at an after-school activity.

5. **Ask your parents to take you to a community event.** Maybe you could go to a movie night at the park or a book reading at the library. Whatever it is, you'll have the chance to meet lots of new people.

Choose the idea that sounds best to you and make a plan to try it this week. Write your plan out below.

But you ARE Brave. You CAN Do this.

Go. Initiate. Invite. Yes, it's awkward to introduce yourself to someone new. It's tough to make new friends. It's scary to put yourself out there. But you *are* brave. You *can* do this.

You don't have to keep feeling lonely. You may be just one chat away from finding the **friend** you've been looking for. You'll never know unless you try.

Did you find the secret message?

Write it out here:

_ _ _ _ _   _ _ _ _ _   _ _

_ _ _ _ _ _ _ _   _ _   _ _

_ _ _ _ _   _ _ _ _ _ _.

3
When It Takes Time to Level Up Your Friendships

"Mom, I need a new book for school."

"Done! It'll be here in two days."

"Dad, wanna watch the new Marvel movie?"

"Sure! Let's watch it tonight on Disney+."

We usually don't have to leave the house to get the things we want. And that's great—most of the time.

The only problem is, we've started to expect everything in life to be fast and easy. And that includes making friends. We want them to show up on our front doorsteps in two days. If it takes longer, we get kind of mad about it.

But **friendship** doesn't come with an ETA (estimated

> *Friendships take a whole lot of time and a whole lot of love.*

time of arrival). There are no shortcuts to deep friendship.

Friendships take a whole lot of time and a whole lot of love. There are about four different "levels" of friendship: (1) girl you know, (2) casual friend, (3) true friend, and (4) best friend. The level you're at often depends on the amount of time you've spent with your friend.

I'm not just talking about time spent sitting next to each other in the classroom. I'm talking about hours and hours spent having fun together—in person.

You may be thinking you'd never have that much time to get to know someone that well. I get it. If you're like me, you haven't had time to clean up your room in . . . well, too long. (Okay, that's a lie. I've had time. I just don't want to.) Or maybe you haven't made time to do other important things, like call your grandparents or play a game with your younger sibling.

The truth is, we'll never have time for anything unless we *make* time. And we have to make time to hang out with our friends if we want those friendships to grow. Hopefully, as the friendships grow, we'll also have a lot of fun.

THE FOUR LEVELS OF
Friendship

Level 1

Girl You Know   This is a girl you see around. Maybe you've seen each other on the school bus or at dance practice. You haven't talked much, but if you're both on social media, you probably follow each other. You may have up to 150 people in your life who fit into this category.

Level 2

Casual Friend   This is a girl you've gotten to know a little. Maybe you're on the same volleyball team or you eat lunch at the same table every day. You might have told her about the books you like or shows you watch—but nothing too serious. You might joke and share laughs, but your conversations are never too deep. You could have up to fifty casual friends.

Level 3

True Friend   This is a girl you know and like who also knows and likes you back. You hang out on weekends. You invite each other to birthday parties. You've probably got an inside joke or two. You may have up to fifteen true friends.

Level 4

Best Friend   This girl feels as close to you as a sister. You've had countless sleepovers and many adventures. She's the first person you tell when you're upset about something, and she's there to celebrate you when you get an A on your math test or win first place at the art show. You can have up to five best friends, but most people only have two.[1]

When I was ten, I started at a new school. By my eleventh birthday, I was still new. And I was still overthinking every single outfit every single day. *Will they be my friends if I wear overalls? Is a blue T-shirt or green T-shirt better?*

My parents encouraged me to have my first birthday party sleepover, and I was terrified. They assured me it would be great. I wasn't convinced, but I wanted to belong so bad that I decided to risk it.

A few girls said yes (*phew!*), but I was still worried that my parents would be weird or my little brother would accidentally walk out of his room in his underwear. So much could go wrong.

The night of the party I made my bed and even cleaned up my clothes pile. My parents made my favorite dinner (baked potatoes), and they bought a *ton* of ice cream. Even though I was scared right up until the girls walked in the door, I did it. I even fought the temptation to pretend to be sick in bed.

They came. We ate food. We giggled. Then we full-on belly laughed. We polished off all the ice cream. We played games. We talked. We stayed up super late. And you know what? That birthday party is still one of my favorites of my whole life. And it was the start of deep and precious friendships with some of those girls.

Also, in case you were worried, none of the things I was

worried about happened, not even my brother making an appearance in his underwear.

My point is that every single friendship has to start somewhere. The friendships that start out awkward and new eventually become something so much more.

They become the girls you talk to about your first crush. The girls who will stand up for you if someone says something behind your back.

They become the girls who cheer you on at dance recitals or on the sidelines at softball games.

They're the girls who pass toilet paper to you under the bathroom stall. The ones who are there to help when you get your first period.

They are the girls whose houses feel like a second home. And who keep your favorite breakfast cereal in the pantry in case you sleep over.

It might not start out perfectly. Between those early days and the days when your friend's parents feel like your own, there is a story. There are those awkward first sleepovers. Then less-awkward sleepovers. Then sleepovers where you make up crazy dance routines and laugh so hard you pee a little. There are movie marathons and concerts. There are summer days at the beach and snowball fights in the winter. There are a million calls and messages.

There's a whole lot of learning to trust that you can be real with each other. There's a lot of telling truths like "I'm having a hard time today" instead of lying and saying, "I'm doing great!" And when those honest moments come, you can be there to cheer each other up.

Sister, believe me, I've been the girl looking out the window and watching the neighbors play together outside. I've been the girl who needed help with her homework but didn't have any friends to ask. I've been the one who doesn't have any close friends at all. The one who was left wondering how other girls got so lucky.

Now I know it wasn't luck; it was time.

What's your Friendship Level?

Think of one friend and answer the following questions.

How do you usually greet each other?

a) I smile and wave but don't say hi.

b) I say hello and talk about something that happened at school.

c) I skip saying hi and jump straight to "Girl, you'll never believe what just happened!"

What emotions do you usually feel when you're around her?

a) I feel happy to see her but a little awkward.

b) I'm just glad she's around.

c) I feel like my day just got a whole lot better!

How much time do you spend together each week?

a) An hour or less—usually not one-on-one.

b) We hang out every week or so.

c) We hang out every weekend—and at school, too, if we can!

What do you like to do together?

a) We usually do whatever our group of friends is doing.

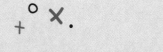

b) We're into the same shows or games and enjoy those together.

c) We do everything together—it's hard to pick one thing!

How do you stay in touch?

a) We just talk whenever we're together.

b) We talk at school and send messages on the weekends.

c) Whether in person or online, we're always in touch somehow.

Have you told her any secrets?

a) Not yet, but maybe someday I will.

b) One or two—and she has shared some too.

c) I've told her *every* secret—there aren't any left to tell!

Would you tell her if you were having a bad day?

a) Maybe, but I wouldn't share any details.

b) Yeah, but then I'd want to change the subject.

c) Yup—and she would hear *all* about it.

Do you wish you were closer with your friend?

a) Yes—I'd like to level up.

b) Yes, but we're already kind of close.

c) I think we're about as close as it gets!

IF YOU GOT MOSTLY A'S:

Then you're casual friends. That's a great place to start—and there's plenty of room for leveling up. If you want to work toward becoming true friends, try reaching out to your friend once a week on the same day just to say hi outside of school. The more opportunities you have to connect, the better you'll get to know each other.

IF YOU GOT MOSTLY B'S:

Then you're true friends. You might be happy staying at the true-friend level. After all, we can only have a small number of best friends. But if you want to level up a true friend into a best friend, try doing something special for her once a week (like bringing an extra cookie to share with her at lunch). Thoughtful, repeated acts of kindness are a great way to let your friend know you care.

IF YOU GOT MOSTLY C'S:

Then you're best friends. You're as close as it gets! There's nowhere to level up from here. But it's important that you still spend time investing in your friendship so it stays strong and healthy. To do this, try making a regular hangout plan to be sure nothing gets in the way of your friendship. For example, you could have a sleepover on the first Saturday of every month.

You might be wondering, *How do I decide who to level up with?* We've already talked about ways to meet new friends. But when it comes to "leveling up" your friendships from a girl you know, to a casual friend, to a true friend, to a best friend, start with someone you already know and like. Maybe she's almost a friend, but you two just haven't reached that next level yet. Maybe she's a neighbor or a girl you sit next to during band practice.

Then pick something you can definitely do. Ask her how you can get in touch outside of school. Ask your parent if you can invite her over for a pizza night. At first it might feel awkward, but that's okay. That's totally normal as you're starting a new friendship.

STICKY NOTE CHALLENGE

Grab a sticky note and write, "You're fun, and I like you!" and sign your name. Then put the note on the locker or desk of a casual friend. It's a small way to let her know you're thinking about her, and you just might turn this casual friend into a true friend!

Whatever you do, start today, sister. Don't wait until tomorrow. Even though starting is always the scariest part, it will get easier. I've been there, and I'm telling you, you can do this. If you try and it doesn't work out, try with someone else. Keep inviting. Keep spending your time on turning a could-be friend into a real-life, can't-wait-to-tell-you-the-crazy-thing-that-just-happened-to-me friend.

If I could go back and talk to the old me, the one who felt all alone, I would take her hands in mine and say, "I'm so, so sorry you're lonely. I know it hurts deeply. Listen, there is nothing wrong with you. You're not broken or unlovable. There is hope. Keep trying and you'll find the friendship of your dreams. Believe in yourself. I know you can do it."

Notes for Your Grown-Up

If you want to share your friendship journey with your grown-up, write some notes from this chapter here.

_____

_____

_____

_____

MAKE A PLAN!

Name one girl you want to try to get closer to this week.

_____

Write one idea for how you might try to grow your friendship with her.

_____

_____

_____

_____

_____

_____

How does your new plan make you feel? Excited?
Hopeful? Scared? Explain why you feel that way.

_____

_____

_____

_____

> REMEMBER, BABY STEPS ARE THE RIGHT SPEED FOR
> SUCCESS. EVERY TIME YOU TAKE A SMALL STEP,
> YOU'RE CLOSER TO HAVING THE FRIENDSHIP YOU'VE
> ALWAYS WANTED. IT'S SO WORTH THE EFFORT.

You're going to have to be brave. And you're going to have to try again and again. It won't be a simple, quick fix. Treat friendship like you would any game or subject in school that you're learning for the very first time. You're not expected to be the best at it right away. But as you keep trying, it gets easier. Soon, that girl you know will become a casual friend. After a little while, that casual friend will become a true friend. Then, a handful of girls' nights later, that true friend may become a best friend.

The journey will be fun!

It's going to be a journey, but the journey will be fun! And it will be worth it.

I want you to know there is hope. So, so, so much hope.

If you're lonely today, know that you might be only a few hangouts away from making your next best friend. All you have to do is keep showing up.

Did you find the secret message?

Write it out here:

_ _ _ _ _ _ _ _

_ _ _ _ _ _ _ _.

4
When You Don't Feel Confident

Sometimes, I do a pretty good job of faking confidence. People will even go so far as to tell me, "Amy, you don't care what anyone thinks. You're so brave."

Ummm. Let's get two things straight here:

1. I care what *everyone* thinks.
2. I question myself all the time. Sometimes even in my sleep.

Most of the time, if you say something nice about me, I'll squirm like a worm, and I'll respond with a list of reasons why I'm not that great.

Anyone: Amy, you look pretty today.

Me: Oh, you're so nice. No. Um . . . I, uh . . . this shirt

has a hole in it. And my messy bun is too messy today. And my hands are so dry and cracked. Do you want to feel my knuckles for proof?

Anyone: Nope. I'm good, but . . . thanks, I think.

Awkward, but I do it almost every time. And maybe you do too. Is this pattern familiar?

Somebody builds you up. You feel weird about it, so you tear yourself down.

This is the opposite of confidence. It's insecurity.

Obviously insecurity isn't healthy. But there's another problem with this response. When you reply negatively, it takes away from the girl who just said the nice thing about you. She might have been trying to break the ice. Maybe this was her way of trying to become friends or level up her friendship with you. And by putting yourself down, you may have put a stop to it. Because it's awkward for the other girl if she feels like her compliment was rejected. And she might not want to risk being rejected by you again.

Just say thank you.

We need to stop doing this. We need to just say thank you and keep chatting. Respond with confidence—not insecurity. You could also try saying something like this:

- "Thanks! You look pretty today too!"
- "That's so nice. Thank **you**!"
- "That makes me really happy!"

BEING
Confident

> **Confidence** (con-fi-dence), *noun*. Knowing you have what it takes to do the things you want to do (like make friends!).

Confidence helps with your . . .

- decision-making skills (because you don't second-guess your choices)
- communication skills (because you're able to say what you mean to say)
- health (because you make choices that are better for you)
- emotions (because it helps you be nicer to yourself)
- friendships (because you're brave enough to try making new friends)
- success (because you're not afraid to try new things)
- safety (because you don't fall for peer pressure)[1]

> **Insecurity** (in-se-cu-ri-ty), *noun*. Feeling like something is wrong with you, like you don't have what it takes to do the things you want to do. This is the opposite of confidence.

Even more important than the way you respond is what you actually *believe*. If you're feeling down about yourself, tell that negative self-talk to take a hike. Look in the mirror and pick out one thing about yourself that makes you feel confident—then choose to focus on that. Maybe you're confident in your sense of humor or your ability to make the most of a blah situation. Whatever it is, believe one nice thing about yourself—and try to let the other things fall away.

I know it can be challenging to believe nice things about ourselves. But if you want to make good friends, you have to start by believing you're a friend worth having.

You might be wondering, *Okay, it's great to be confident. But how will that help me make friends?* Here **are** five ways you can use confidence to make and grow your friendships:

1. **Give compliments.** Confident girls never need to tear someone else down to feel better about themselves. Instead, they're happy to boost other girls up.
2. **Ask questions.** Rather than trying to impress their friends, confident girls try to *know* their friends. They ask them what they like to eat. They ask them about their dreams for the future. They ask them where they bought their pink backpack. They are curious to know their friends better.

3. **Be a good listener.** Once they've asked all those questions, confident girls listen for the response! Confidence means you don't always have to be the one talking.

4. **Set the phone aside.** Confident girls don't need to know what's happening on social media every second. They're not thinking about FOMO (fear of missing out). They're able to enjoy the people they're hanging out with in real time.

5. **Be okay with silence.** It's normal! Confident girls are okay with a pause in conversation. Think of a new question to ask. Or just sit in silence for a moment. It's okay!

Do you want to know something I do when I'm *not* feeling so confident?

I talk. I talk a lot.

Actually, I talk a lot no matter what. Maybe it's because I'm an only child, so I never had anyone to talk to or play with at home. Or maybe I just didn't have a sibling to tell me to stop talking so much. I dunno, but I know it's worse when I'm nervous. Sometimes people think I talk so much because I'm confident. But that is *so* not true.

BOOST YOUR CONFIDENCE!

Write a letter to yourself about why you're great. Memorize it. Repeat it before you walk into school in the morning. Say it anytime you need a boost. Here's an example:

Dear Amy,

There is nothing wrong with you.

You are special and unique. You're a good friend who makes other people laugh. You know how to have a fun time. You can be confident today because you are a friend worth having.

Keep being yourself. Keep being good to others. And good friendships will come.

Love, Amy

Now it's your turn!

For example, maybe I'm being loud and fun at a birthday party, doing things like this:

- Showing off TikTok dance moves
- Singing all the parts to "We Don't Talk About Bruno"
- Making jokes (Did you hear about the bear who lost all his teeth? He was a *gummy bear*. Ha!)
- Telling new people about the time I walked all over Target with a giant hole in my pants and nobody told me my underwear was hanging out

But this is what I'm really thinking:

- *I hope they like me.*
- *I hope they don't talk bad about me later.*
- *I hope they want to be my friend.*
- *I hope I'm not doing anything weird with my hands. Like, am I using them enough? Too much? Should they be in my pockets? Oh, I'm wearing leggings; I don't even have pockets. Do I clasp them together? Put them on my belly? No, that's strange. On my hips? Do they always just dangle like this?*

Instead of being truly confident, I'm faking it. I'm

pretending. And ultimately, that doesn't make me feel good. It also means other girls have a harder time getting to know the real me.

You know where I fake confidence the most? On social media. I'm always posting photos or videos that make me look cool and calm and confident. But really, I'm just hoping that the photos will make other people *think* I'm cool and calm and confident. And when I don't get as many likes or comments as I want, I feel worse about myself. I feel like no one wants to be my **friend**.

But getting—or not getting—the social media comments and likes isn't the only problem. Some girls feel insecure because they don't have any social media accounts at all. Maybe their parents won't let them, or maybe they just don't want them. But then they worry that if they don't have a TikTok or YouTube or Snapchat account, other girls won't want to be their friends, or they'll miss out on important things.

Here's the thing: real friendship isn't about social media. Like, *at all*. Real friendship happens when you spend time together—*in person*. Real friendship is saying, "I love your face. No, actually, I love *looking* at your face."

Social media is the opposite of that. When you're always on your phone, you're not spending time face-to-face with your friends. And remember when I said that you have to have confidence to make good friends? Well, social media can kill your confidence.

Unfortunately, social media often leads to depression and anxiety. Check out these facts:

- Social media use causes feelings of depression, insecurity, anxiety, comparison, jealousy, loneliness, and FOMO.
- Social media can lead to cyberbullying, isolation, ADHD, dangerous activities, bad sleep, and addiction.[2]

These are long lists of some really hard stuff to tackle. But you don't have to just accept it as part of life. If social media is killing your confidence, there are some things you can do to help:

1. **Change your social media feed.** Are you following a lot of influencers who make you feel bad about your life in some way? Maybe you wish you looked like them, had as much money as they did, or could dance or sing like them. If the answer is yes, unfollow those accounts. Seriously! If you don't feel

WHAT'S UP WITH SOCIAL MEDIA?

FOR TWEENS
(AGES 8–12):

38%	100%

38% USE SOCIAL MEDIA

18% USE SOCIAL MEDIA EVERY DAY

GIRLS SPEND ALMOST

5 HOURS PER DAY

ON SCREENS FOR FUN
(TV, TABLETS, COMPUTERS, MOBILE PHONES)

GIRLS SPEND ALMOST

30 MINUTES PER DAY

ON SOCIAL MEDIA

FOR TEENS
(AGES 13–18):

84%	100%

84% USE SOCIAL MEDIA

62% USE SOCIAL MEDIA EVERY DAY

GIRLS SPEND ALMOST

8 HOURS PER DAY

ON SCREENS FOR FUN
(TV, TABLETS, COMPUTERS, MOBILE PHONES)

GIRLS SPEND ALMOST

1 HOUR AND 30 MINUTES PER DAY

ON SOCIAL MEDIA[3]

good about yourself when you look at their posts, then don't look. You'll be happier if you make these changes, and who doesn't want that?

2. **Spend less time on social media.** You don't have to stop using it altogether (unless your parents say so). But research shows that the more time you spend on social media, the more likely you are to experience some harmful side effects: FOMO, unrealistic expectations, depression, insecurity, comparison, jealousy, and tech addiction. And really, do you want to be a FOMO person or a JOMO (joy of missing out) person?

3. **Focus on your own lane.** Think about three things in your life that are bringing you joy right now. Maybe you're crushing it in your math class at school. Or you're getting a lot better at piano. Or you love the new shirt you bought online. Or your friends are awesome. Or you got a new puppy. Whatever the three things are, remind yourself of those things, and don't compare them to anything else. And as tempting as it is to share exciting things on social media, keep in mind that when you do, it might cause others to compare themselves to you. Just focus on being you and loving the life you're living.

STICKY NOTE CHALLENGE

Grab a sticky note and write three things you like about yourself. Put it next to your computer or on the back side of your phone or tablet. The next time you're watching videos or scrolling social media, look at your note and remember that you don't need to be like anyone else. You don't need to impress anyone else either. You are great just the way you are!

4. **Remember the filter.** Always remember that on social media, you're not looking at people. You're looking at pictures of people. Filtered pictures. Whenever you see a photo of someone on social media and experience feelings of jealousy, ask yourself, What is her life like without the filter? Spoiler alert: you don't know the answer! You're seeing only a small, filtered snippet of her life. Always keep that in mind to avoid comparing your real life to someone's filtered photos.

5. **Ignore the likes.** It's so easy to believe that the

more likes you get on social media, the more loved you are, but it's not true. Remember, more likes simply means a lot of people clicked a little button on that post—and does that really matter? Nah. Getting more likes doesn't mean you have a better life or you're a better person or a better friend. Truly. It doesn't mean anything, and it's never where your **worth** or your confidence should come from.

Okay, so we've talked about how confidence can help you make friends. And we've talked about how social media can kill your confidence—so you have a harder time making friends. But there's one other important thing that confidence can do: it can help you *keep* friends.

When you feel insecure—which is the opposite of confident—sometimes, you get clingy. You start to worry when your friend makes a new friend. *Does she like her better than me? Will she stop wanting to be my friend now? Am I less cool? How can I force my way back to the top of my friend's list?*

That isn't fair to them, and it's not fair to you either. Who says you can only have one close friend? Who says you can't hang out with one friend on Saturday and a different friend on Sunday? And who knows—maybe her new friend could become a new friend for you too.

Notes for Your Grown-Up

If you want to share your friendship journey with your grown-up, write some notes from this chapter here.

_____

_____

_____

_____

_____

_____

_____

_____

_____

_____

_____

_____

You'll find the friends who love you just the way you are.

It can become tiring trying to always prove that you're good enough. As though friendship is a game where there's only one winner and everyone else loses.

If anything, friendship needs to be treated as the type of game where everyone works together and is better as part of a team.

When you're confident, you don't worry so much about fitting in. You're okay with standing out and being real. And being your true self is a must if you want to have good friends. When you are your true self, you'll find the friends who love you just the way you are.

You are **great**. Your friends think so too.

So get out there. Stand tall and have confidence.

Did you find the secret message?

Write it out here:

_ _ _ _   _ _ _ _ _

_ _ _ _ _   _ _ _ _ _ _ _ .

5

When You're Pretty Sure You've Been Tricked

When I was ten years old, I had a best friend who made life like a movie. He told the best stories. And the thing is, I always believed him—even when the stories were clearly made up.

FRIEND: See that horse over there? It used to live up in the mountains. But then it got stolen by a rodeo clown. And then the clown sold the horse for money. So now the horse lives in this field.

ME: What?! That's so crazy! How did you know that?

FRIEND: Can you see the fairies in the trees over there?

ME: What?! No. Where are they? Why can't I see them?

> **FRIEND:** I saw bear prints in our fort the other day.
>
> **ME:** What?! Are you serious? That's so scary! We need to tell someone!

One day when we were playing outside, he dared me to taste a plant he'd pulled out of the ground. "It's really good for you," he said. "You're not scared, are you?" He took a big bite and grinned at me while he chewed it.

I glared at him. "I'm *not* scared," I said. I didn't break eye contact as I ate the plant. After I'd swallowed it, his eyes got big. "I accidentally gave you the wrong plant," he said, trying to trick me. "That's the poisonous one."

"Yeah right," I said. "Besides, you ate it too."

"I'm immune to it," he explained. "It can't poison me."

Then his mom called for him, and he ran off. I stood there, frozen, with the plant hanging from my hand.

"I don't believe you!" I shouted after him.

"See ya!" he called over his shoulder.

"I don't believe you!"

I spent the rest of the evening spitting. I was spitting as I walked to the house. Then I sat on the porch and started spitting some more. I figured this might be my last day on earth, and spitting was my best chance at survival. My mom came out to ask me why I spitting all over her flowers. I told her what had happened. I felt like I was going to cry.

"Which plant?" she asked. I showed her, and she laughed. "You're fine, hon. He was teasing you. Those are just carrot greens."

Well played, buddy. Well played.

The thing is, it's pretty easy to trick me, even today. I'm gullible. Which is why I've fallen for so many lies over the years—especially lies about friendship. These lies kept me feeling all alone. They made me believe that I had to have lots of followers to have friends. That I had to have the coolest new toys or video game systems. That I was the only one who didn't have anyone to sit with at lunch. That it was impossible to make new friends.

Now that I know the truth, I want to tell other girls so they don't believe these same lies. If you have been tricked by any of the lies in this list, it's time to kick them to the curb and replace them with the truth.

LIE #1: YOU HAVE TO BE POPULAR TO HAVE FRIENDS

We've been fed this lie since preschool. It makes us think, *If I'm pretty enough, sporty enough, or funny enough, then everyone will like me. If I'm enough, I'll belong. If I'm enough,*

I'll be loved. If I'm enough, I'll have friends. If I'm enough, I'll be invited. If you're like me, you've always kind of known that these "enoughs" aren't true. But you still try to be "enough" in all of these areas—just in case. Maybe you think that to fix your loneliness, all you have to do is start shopping at Forever 21. Or have a birthday party at Sky Zone. Or be the MVP (most valuable player) in dodgeball.

You are enough as you are.

Listen, friend: the idea that you're not enough is a big fat lie. I know it, and you know it, so let's stop believing it. You are enough as you are, and so am I. We don't need to be prettier, smaller, stronger, or anything other than as we are. Those are poisonous thoughts.

LIE #2: YOU CAN HAVE GOOD FRIENDS WITHOUT BEING A GOOD FRIEND

This lie applies to when you never message back, never make time to hang out, always wait for your friend to initiate hanging out, or flake on plans. There are memes that say things like, "I might never text you back, but I still love you." That's not what it means to be a good friend. How would you feel if your friend never got ahold of you? You'd probably feel like you weren't really friends.

We Can Stop Bullying

17% OF KIDS REPORT BEING BULLIED TWO OR MORE TIMES PER MONTH

160,000 KIDS STAY HOME FROM SCHOOL EACH DAY BECAUSE OF BULLYING

girls ARE MORE LIKELY THAN BOYS TO EXPERIENCE CYBERBULLYING

girls ARE MORE LIKELY TO EXPERIENCE SOCIAL BULLYING

64% OF KIDS WHO ARE BULLIED DON'T REPORT IT

OVER **90%** OF STUDENTS DON'T LIKE TO SEE ANOTHER KID BEING BULLIED

BUT LESS THAN **20%** OF KIDS TRY TO STOP BULLYING WHEN THEY SEE IT HAPPEN

Over half OF BULLIES STOP WHEN ANOTHER KID STEPS IN

Be a Defender

When kids see another kid being bullied, they take on one of four roles:

1. **Outsiders:** they don't do anything
2. **Defenders:** they offer to help the person being bullied
3. **Reinforcers:** they laugh or encourage the bully
4. **Assistants:** they take part in the bullying[1]

WE SHOULD ALL BE DEFENDERS!

HERE'S HOW:

STOP BULLYING BEFORE IT HAPPENS.

INVITE KIDS WHO ARE LEFT OUT TO WALK WITH YOU IN THE HALLWAY OR SIT WITH YOU AT LUNCH.

CALL A BULLY OUT.

IT COULD BE AS SIMPLE AS ASKING, "WHAT ARE YOU DOING?" OR SAYING, "THAT'S NOT FUNNY."

Be KIND AND RESPECTFUL.

ACT THIS WAY TOWARD EVERYONE—EVEN PEOPLE YOU DISAGREE WITH.

DISAGREE WITH A BULLY.

YOU MIGHT SAY SOMETHING LIKE, "I ACTUALLY THINK SHE'S REALLY COOL."

TELL A TRUSTED ADULT.

COUNSELOR'S Office

WHEN YOU SEE SOMEONE BEING BULLIED, TELL A PARENT, TEACHER, OR OTHER TRUSTED ADULT TO KEEP IT FROM HAPPENING AGAIN.

The thing is, you **can** be a bad friend on accident. We'll talk about that in another chapter. But let's at least be sure we're not trying to be bad friends on purpose.

Good friendships take effort. You can't be a bad friend and expect to have good friendships. You just can't. You can't expect to create deep friendships if you always watch what you want to watch, play the games that you want to play, and hang out when you want to hang out. You can't take and take and take. You can't treat people like they don't matter to you if you want to matter to them. That's just not the way things work—in friendship or in life.

We're talking about the Golden Rule here: "Treat others the way you want to be treated." If you don't live by this rule, you risk becoming someone who bullies others to get her own way. Be better than that. Be the kind of girl who stands up for others, even if they aren't your friends. Then you'll always be a friend worth having!

LIE #3: YOU DON'T REALLY NEED FRIENDS

Sometimes we act like we can go through life all alone, like we don't need anyone else. Like having friends isn't a necessity; it's just a "bonus." But friendship isn't a bonus; we *need* friends. We need to belong. And friendship is a really big part of belonging. Which is why we spend so much time trying to make new friends or level up the ones we already have.

It's why we might choose to ride bikes around **the** block with our friends instead of watching one more episode of *iCarly*. Or why we might put down a good book during lunch so we can talk to someone new in the school cafeteria. Or why we might spend time playing a new sport or learning a new activity instead of sitting at home, staring at a screen. Friendship is important, so we need to treat it like it's important.

We don't just want friendship. We need it.

THE TRUTH

We've been sold a lot of half-truths and straight-up **lies** when it comes to friendship, but the good news is that the truth is even better than we expected.

The truth, my friend, is that you are enough exactly as you are. The truth is that real friendship is not a popularity contest. The truth is that making time for your friends matters a whole lot. The truth is, you don't have to wait for a friend to magically pop into your life. You have the power to go out **and find** new friends. And you can get started today!

A Good Friend Makes You Feel...

Find and circle all the words hidden in the grid below.
Remember to look in every direction!

HAPPY

CONFIDENT

ADVENTUROUS

SAFE

EXCITED

CALM

CHEERFUL

HOPEFUL[2]

```
V X U P K H O P E F U L E N F
E O D F I I Z S B N V K K P I
C O N F I D E N T V I B R W C
T G F O D M P S C X B V N P W
E N R Q E X R D H K U M U V G
O X I S N C Q S V M L K H S M
T E C H E E R F U L Z E A P R
F B Z I I B F Z C Q O Q P S L
D G R Q T D B E E P N M P D D
C U J R L E R C M K G D Y K M
A H J S R Z D M N G O J M M Z
T Y Z A N O Z W Z C A L M V J
G P P F A E C P V V X Y D C A
A D V E N T U R O U S H V B S
H R H D R Y Z V H B H R F W R
```

DITCH THE LIES!

Jot down some lies you've believed about friendship
(maybe they're in this chapter, maybe they're not).
Circle the one that has stuck with you and bothered
you the most. Then write a letter to yourself with the
truth. Here's the letter I would write to myself:

Dear Jess,

I know you often feel like you're not enough. I know
you often believe the lie that you aren't lovable as you
are. But you are enough. You are beautiful. You are
loved. You are worthy. As. You. Are. The end.

I'm going to say something to you that you really
need to hear: stop trying so hard. Stop trying to change
yourself. Instead, go out there and find someone who
needs a friend like you. Love someone else as they
are—someone who will love you as you are.

You've got this. You really do.

Love, Jess

Now it's your turn!

_____

_____

_____

_____

_____

_____

_____

_____

_____

_____

_____

_____

_____

_____

_____

_____

Notes for Your Grown-Up

If you want to share your friendship journey with your grown-up, write some notes from this chapter here.

_____

_____

_____

_____

_____

_____

_____

_____

_____

_____

_____

_____

Let's start focusing on these truths about friendship and forget the lies. And while we're at it, here are three other truths to keep in mind as you continue your friendship journey.

1. **They're not you.** If you get one thing from this book, let it be this: other people are not you. They don't think like you. They don't feel like you. They don't care about the same things you care about. We can't force people to be just like us. We have to allow them the freedom to be themselves. Yes, sometimes this makes friendship harder, but it also makes friendship more interesting, fun, and beautiful.

2. **You'll always find what you're looking for.** Listen up. If you expect people to reject you, fail you, or be mean and hurtful, you're going to find what you're looking for. If you walk through life thinking, *Every girl is stuck-up*, do you know what you're going to find? Only mean girls. Learn to look for the good— really, really look for it—and you'll most likely find what you're looking for.

3. **It's normal to feel awkward when you're making new friends.** Sweaty palms? Itchy neck? Talking too much? Can't think of *anything* to say?

Wondering if you're weird and then thinking that, yep, you're definitely weird? All normal. When you're getting to know someone, it's awkward. And you're not alone—we all feel this way! So go into a new friendship expecting it to be kind of weird at first. Your friendship will get more comfortable with time.

The friendships we long for aren't impossible to find; they may actually be very close by. Let's stop believing the lies we've heard about **friendship** and start listening to the truth. When we do, we might find that the friends we've been looking for are right around the corner.

STICKY NOTE CHALLENGE

Pick one of the truths listed in this chapter—whichever one feels most important to you right now. Write it on a sticky note and place it on your nightstand or near your bed. Each night, go to sleep with that truth in your mind and dream about the kind of real friendship you deserve.

WHEN YOU'RE PRETTY SURE YOU'VE BEEN TRICKED

Did you find the secret message?

Write it out here:

73

6
When Someone Doesn't Like You

There is this girl I know who doesn't like me.

I've tried. Truly. I once baked her homemade chocolate chip cookies. I've invited her to come to the mall with me. I've given her lots of compliments. "Oh my gosh, I love your shirt. You look so cute in purple."

But still, I can tell she doesn't like me—maybe because I'm trying way too hard. But I'd argue that I'm being nice! Please like me back and give me compliments! Isn't that the way the world is supposed to work?

Even so, I can tell she wants to sneak away anytime we talk. And for whatever reason, I still want to grab her by the sleeve and force her to stay so she can finally learn how great I am.

I really don't know why she doesn't like me. As far as I

75

know, I haven't done anything to offend, annoy, or hurt her. And I definitely haven't done anything on purpose. I really enjoy her as a friend.

I used to think about this a lot. It really bothered me.

Then a few months ago, do **you** know what I found out? It was all in my head.

I'd made the whole thing up.

She was crazy about me. Big fan. Big. Huge.

Nah, I'm just kidding. I found out she really does not like me at all.

> **What matters is how we react.**

I wish this story were like one of those cutesy, oh-my-goodness-we-actually-became-best-friends shows you watch on Netflix. Those stories **are** sweet, but that's not always the way it goes. Sometimes, people don't like us. And it doesn't really matter why. What matters is how we react when people don't like us.

I think we all have our big "thing." You know, something we struggle with. Something we do to get people to like us. We probably can't remember how or why we started doing this "thing" in the first place. But it's there. It's like an automatic response now. **A** reflex.

Mine is people pleasing. Which basically means that everything I do screams, "Please just like me!"

It also means I don't stand up for myself. I say yes when I want to say no. I get mad when I think someone is wrong, but I don't speak up and share my thoughts. I "go with the flow" even when the flow feels like it's going in a bad direction. And I assume people are mad at me all the time. If you're going to be my friend, I'm going to need you to text me here and there with a random "Hey, Ames, just letting you know I'm not mad at you. Okay, love you. Bye." (Kidding!)

I could literally be handing out warm, gooey, delicious chocolate chip cookies, and in my head, I'd still be thinking, *I hope these don't taste like burned pieces of Play-Doh. I hope they don't make anyone sick. Oh my goodness. These chocolate chip cookies were a bad idea. Why did I do this? No one is ever going to want to be my friend again if these are gross.*

Listen. Chocolate chip cookies are never a bad idea. But sometimes I try so hard to people please that I lose all common sense.

Maybe your reflex isn't people pleasing. Maybe it's one of these:

- Trying to do everything perfectly
- Thinking of only worst-case scenarios
- Competing with others to an extreme degree

It's almost like we're all trying to prove something to the world. Like, "Here. Look at this. I did it! I really do matter, world." But you matter even if people aren't happy with you. You matter even if you don't do things perfectly. You matter even if you don't come in first. You matter even if you still don't get invited to that party or you don't have fun plans for the weekend.

More than seven billion people live on this planet. Of course they don't all like you. And on a smaller level, not all the people who go to your school or live in your neighborhood or are on your sports team or are in your Girl Scout troop are going to like you. It doesn't mean you're doing something wrong. It's just a fact of life.

I like to believe that one day, I'll wake up and I won't care what anyone thinks about me anymore. I'll dye my hair pink, and I'll walk around wearing giant sunglasses indoors like a celebrity. I won't mind so much if someone argues with my opinion or doesn't like what I have to say. I won't stay up and wonder why I wasn't invited, and I won't try so hard to go with the flow.

But until that happens, there are a few things I can do.

First, I can learn to recognize the "thing" I do to get people to like me, my reflex. When I get nervous about meeting someone new, when I'm trying to convince someone to like me, or when I'm not being my most confident self, I become a people pleaser. Here are the signs:

- Always agreeing with everyone
- Saying sorry for things that aren't my fault
- Never sharing my opinion with others
- Saying I'm fine when I'm actually upset
- Never being proud of myself until other people say they're proud of me
- Saying yes to things I don't actually want to do
- Not standing up for myself

If I catch myself thinking or doing any of these things, I know I need to make a change.

Then I can find the good in my instinctive behavior, or "thing" that I deal with. Just like almost everything in life, it has good parts as well as bad parts. We've already talked about the bad parts. But here are some good parts to my people pleasing:

WE ALL HAVE A "thing"

WANTING TO MAKE EVERYONE ELSE HAPPY MORE THAN YOU WANT TO MAKE YOURSELF HAPPY

UP TO 54% OF FEMALES STRUGGLE WITH PEOPLE PLEASING

PEOPLE PLEASING

PEOPLE PLEASERS ARE MORE LIKELY TO . . .
- Get bullied
- Cave in to peer pressure
- Become part of a clique[1]

WANTING TO DO EVERYTHING THE "RIGHT" WAY AND NEVER MAKE ANY MISTAKES

✓ ✓ ✓

PERFECTIONISM

UP TO 30% OF KIDS STRUGGLE WITH PERFECTIONISM

PERFECTIONISTS ARE MORE LIKELY TO . . .
- Think that they failed at something
- Tattle on others
- Criticize others[2]

WORRYING ABOUT ALL THE WAYS SOMETHING COULD GO WRONG OR TURN BAD

UP TO 14% OF KIDS STRUGGLE WITH ANXIETY OR DEPRESSION, WHICH CAN CAUSE WORST-CASE-SCENARIO THINKING

WORST-CASE-SCENARIO THINKERS ARE MORE LIKELY TO . . .
- Worry about things
- Assume the worst in others
- Have a big reaction to a small problem[3]

WANTING TO DO BETTER THAN EVERYONE ELSE AND "WIN" AT LIFE

UP TO 49% OF STUDENTS FEEL STRESS EVERY DAY, WHICH CAN BE CAUSED BY FEELING THE NEED TO CONSTANTLY COMPETE

OVERLY COMPETITIVE KIDS ARE MORE LIKELY TO . . .
- Feel pressure to be the best
- Feel frustrated when faced with a challenge
- Get overwhelmed by school and activities[4]

- I always consider other people's feelings.
- I notice when my friends need help with something.
- I don't get angry easily.
- I'm good at including everyone.

These all help me to be a good friend. If I keep these good parts and remove the bad, my "thing" doesn't have to be bad at all. And other "things" have their upsides too. Perfectionism means I have a strong sense of integrity. Worse-case-scenario thinking means I am great at making plans. Constantly competing with others means I am a hard worker and always trying to do my best.

And finally, I can fight against the bad parts of my "thing." When I catch myself worrying too much about what other people think of me, I can stop those thoughts in their tracks. I can tell myself all the things that are good about me.

One day, I went to Chick-fil-A for some fine dining on waffle fries and chicken nuggets. And I realized something big: I can't be everyone's Chick-fil-A sauce. Those six little words changed everything for me. Let me explain.

While I was enjoying my feast, I looked around and noticed something strange. On one woman's tray, I saw ketchup and ranch. At another table, I saw packets of barbecue, Polynesian, and honey mustard sauce. I had chosen Chick-fil-A sauce because—let's be serious—it's the best one. I can't understand why anyone would want anything else, but that's the thing: people aren't the same.

Everyone chooses differently. Everyone wants and needs different things. Everyone brings different things to the table. Nobody is the same. And this is true of both chicken nugget sauce and friendships.

There is no one thing that makes someone a good friend. So I probably shouldn't take it so personally when someone doesn't like me. I can't be everyone's bestie. I can't be invited to every single Halloween party. I can't be everyone's Chick-fil-A sauce. And neither can you.

For some people, you are going to be too salty. For others, you're going to be too sweet. You will be both too much and not enough for some people's taste buds. And that's okay.

Your flavor is uniquely you. It won't be for everyone. But that doesn't make it any less great.

It's not your job to make everyone like you. Your job is to do what no one else can: be yourself.

Your flavor is uniquely you.

WHAT IS YOUR "THING"?

Are you a people pleaser? A perfectionist? A worst-case-scenario thinker? An overly competitive person? Or something else?

_____

_____

What are the bad parts about it?

_____

_____

_____

_____

What are the good parts about it?

_____

_____

_____

_____

What is one good part you can focus on this week to help you be a better friend?

_____

_____

_____

_____

What's your Friendship Flavor?

How many best friends do you have?

a) None yet, but I've got lots of true friends

b) Just one—and she's the best

c) Two or three—and they don't know each other

d) Three to five

e) Too many to count!

The perfect sleepover would include . . .

a) Just me and a great book

b) A movie marathon with my best friend

c) A clothing-swap party followed by a dance party

d) Something everyone will enjoy: pizza, games, and a ton of candy

e) Anything—as long as all of my friends are there

Which emoji best represents you?

a) Book/reading emoji

b) Red-heart emoji

c) Thumbs-up emoji

d) Face-with-tears-of-joy emoji

e) Party-popper emoji

When you grow up, you want to be . . .

a) A writer

b) A therapist

c) A traveling photographer

d) A nurse

e) A social media influencer

What's one word your friends use to describe you?

a) Thoughtful

b) Caring

c) Outgoing

d) Reliable

e) Excitable[5]

IF YOU GOT MOSTLY A'S:

Your friendship flavor is ketchup! You're a classic gal who can get along with anyone but isn't afraid to do her own thing. Your friends love that you're so independent—and that you always have the best book recommendations.

IF YOU GOT MOSTLY B'S:

Your friendship flavor is honey mustard! You're sweet and straightforward, and you'd choose hanging out one-on-one with your bestie over a big group thing any day. Your friends love that you're a great listener who knows them so well.

IF YOU GOT MOSTLY C'S:

Your friendship flavor is barbecue! You're a tangy mix of flavors that work together to create something amazing. Your friends love that you're always trying new styles and recommending unique activities and games. They love that you have so many different interests—it keeps them on their toes!

IF YOU GOT MOSTLY D'S:

Your friendship flavor is ranch dressing! You're the kind of girl who blends well with lots of different flavors, and your friends know they can always count on you. You help people feel welcome, and you know just what to do to make someone's day better. Your friend group simply wouldn't be the same without you.

IF YOU GOT MOSTLY E'S:

Your friendship flavor is hot sauce! You're bold and spicy and always looking for a good time. Your friends love that you're not afraid to be yourself and that you're always ready to hang out— even if they might need some convincing first.

STICKY NOTE CHALLENGE

Grab a sticky note and write, "_____ is amazing." Fill in the blank with whatever type of sauce represents you! Then put the sticky note on your refrigerator so you'll always remember that your unique flavor is especially great (even if it's not for everyone).

And yet, sometimes people just don't like other people for no real reason at all. I understand if that hurts your feelings. It hurts my feelings a little too. But when **you** are showing up and being authentic, you'll find friends who like you for you, and that is one of the sweetest gifts in life.

So go. Walk into rooms with your head held high. Embrace your quirks and your personality. Embrace your talents and your hobbies and your sense of humor and all the million little things that make you unique. Embrace your flavor. It's a good one.

Here are a few reminders. Highlight them. Memorize them. Do whatever you've got to do so you'll never forget them:

- Your friends will accept you for who you are and know your heart is in the right place.
- Your friends will love you because of your personality, your hobbies, your ideas, and your opinions.
- Your friends won't mind being told no every once in a while because they'll understand what's important to you.
- Your friends will want to know the real you—not the you that is driven by your insecurities.

Notes for Your Grown-Up

If you want to share your friendship journey with your grown-up, write some notes from this chapter here.

_____

_____

_____

_____

If you want to be a good friend, you have to be yourself. Not everyone will like you. It isn't something you can force. So instead of trying to control how somebody else feels about you, control what you put out there. Make sure it's a lot of love, then rest easy, friend. You did what you could. You **are** who you are. And that will always be enough.

Did you find the secret message?

Write it out here:

7
When Everyone Seems Fake

I need my friendships to be real and real only. I mean it. I'd rather run a mile during gym class than be stuck having surface-level conversations about homework or the weather or what's for lunch.

Listen, if I'm hanging out with my friends, I don't want to be stuck in the shallow end of the pool. Don't get me wrong, snort laughing about the weird dream you had last night counts. I'm not saying everything needs to be serious. But I am saying we're all the superheroes of our own stories. But when we're finished fighting crime and we come together in the Avengers headquarters, we need to **take** off our masks and just be.

I want to be real with my friends. And I want them to be real with me too.

I want to make friendship bracelets together and not worry if what I'm making is kind of ugly or a little uneven. Friendship should be the place where we don't have to hide our mistakes or feel embarrassed. It should be the place where we come as we are and snuggle up in our sleeping bags and share what we're excited about and what we're afraid of. It should be the place where we can eat brownie batter right out of the bowl and lick the last bits off our fingers. It should be the place where we feel like we belong.

The sad thing is that most of us have experienced the opposite of that. We've heard girls say mean things in the bathroom. We've been left out because we didn't look the "right" way. We've been judged because we weren't good at sports or math or singing or video games. We've stood awkwardly and listened while other girls gossiped and said mean things. And we've wondered what they must say about us behind our backs.

We've been taught not to invite people into our mess. We've been taught to hide.

We've been taught to hide our flaws by putting a filter over our photos and videos.

We've been taught to only show up on-screen with a ring light and a good angle.

We've been taught to clean our rooms before our friends

come over so they won't see our stack of nerdy comics or our dirty laundry or our crumpled-up homework assignments.

We've held back our tears.

We've thought, *Is this just how it is?*

Deep down, though, we know there's something better.

Listen, friend: real friendship is rare. But it's not impossible.

I moved a lot as a kid, and each time felt like a tryout for friendship. I tried so hard to figure out who I needed to be at this new school to be accepted. All I wanted was to belong. But the more I tried to belong, the less I acted like myself. I tried to say the right things, wear the right things, and be into the right things. I changed my wardrobe depending on what was cool at the new school. Maybe I wore jeans and oversized T-shirts at one school. Then I'd switch to leggings and athletic tops at another. Although some of that was true to me, I was only showing the parts of me I thought other kids would like.

I will never forget being in a classroom full of people and still feeling very much alone. I will never forget looking around the lunchroom and panicking because there was no place where I felt invited to sit. I will never forget sneaking past the hallway monitors just so I could lock myself in a bathroom stall until the lunch period was over.

HOW TO MAKE FRIENDSHIP BRACELETS

What you need:

- RULER
- STRING (4 DIFFERENT COLORS)
- SCISSORS
- TAPE
- BEADS (OPTIONAL)

Directions:

1. Grab the ruler and measure each string to 40 inches.

2. Use the scissors to cut each string to that length.

3. Collect all the strings together, then pull the threads in half and make a knot with a loop in the middle.

4. Tape the loop to a table, book, or any other surface so the threads stay in place.

5. Separate the threads into two sets: one of each color on each side. There should be four strings on the left and four on the right.

6. Arrange the threads in a mirror image of each other, so the same color threads are on the outside and the same color threads are on the inside. See image A.

7. Now take the outside string on the left set and bring it to the inside of the right set. See image B.

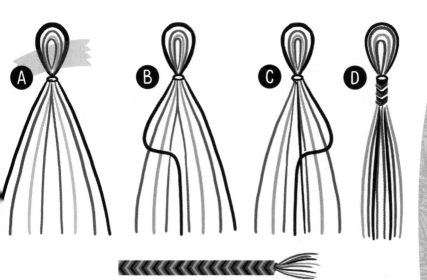

8. Then do the same thing on the other side: take the outside string on the right set and bring it to the inside of the left set. See image C.

9. Keep doing this until every color has crossed over. This creates a "fishtail" knot.

10. Tighten the knot by pulling on the strings. See image D.

> **Optional:** As you braid, you can add in beads. Loop the strings through the beads to secure them. Try adding 1 bead every ½ inch on the bracelet.

11. Continue until you make it to the end of the string.

12. Finish the braid by tying a knot at the end.

THEN ASK YOUR FRIEND TO TIE THE BRACELET ONTO YOUR WRIST![1]

Friendship shouldn't feel like squeezing yourself into a box. Friendship can be a sacred place. But we need to let down our guard, let others in (like, really in), and let ourselves be known and seen—mess and all.

Hear me when I say this: your mess doesn't make you unfriendable. It's actually the opposite. If you invite people into your mess, you're creating space for them to have their mess too. I know exactly zero people who don't have some mess—**and** I'm not just talking about messy rooms or lockers or desks. Maybe their mess is more like one of these situations:

- A bad relationship with their older sibling
- Anxiety or depression
- A health condition
- Feeling insecure or being super shy
- Having to move around a lot with their family
- Trouble focusing in school

We all have messes.

There are only two ways to deal with mess. We can accept it and be real about it, or we can be embarrassed about it and hide it. The first one can lead to real, great friendships. The second one leads to loneliness.

Real Friendships Are ...

Find and circle all the words hidden in the grid below.
Remember to look in every direction!

NONJUDGMENTAL   SUPPORTIVE   SISTERLY

INVITING   OPEN   SWEET

ENCOURAGING   EXCITING

V E A L V V B Z C A Z E D F K
V S X K F C G E N S M N P Z B
L U Z C P U T R O U Q C J O W
K P P Q I F Z Y N A J O H U A
L P I M Y T M I J W P U T B P
Y O N B S Z I O U C V R I Y G
M R V V O I L N D H B A G K R
D T I P G Q S V G B T G T J R
H I T D A N E T M E N I T A S
Q V I P S G Y Y E U F N E O M
P E N E V T Z W N R V G A P J
E B G N S X S L T J L X A E P
G T G M C Z U Z A B R Y D N C
M I U B M C V U L R N D X B V
B F N A L Y V H D G X T V X S

It's time to drop the fake act and be real. Then we'll have the confidence to know that we belong—no matter what.

One day, I was sitting in a friend's living room and I just let it all spill. All my struggles, all my fears, and all my I-don't-know-how-to-do-this frustrations. All of my insecurities about feeling like I was the only kid who didn't belong or fit in. All of my mess. I was like a bottle of Coke that had been shaken up so much it finally exploded. My friends listened calmly. They asked questions. Then they said the thing I needed to hear: "I totally get it; I've been there."

Is there anything better than that? Is there anything better than hearing "me too" or "I've been there" or "I'm here"? Is there anything better than getting all those pent-up feelings out on the table and being loved and accepted for who you are and where you are? Is there anything better than being truly known without secrets? Is there anything better than not being lonely anymore?

I don't know if there is.

When you open up your heart and are met with love, it's the greatest experience.

In friendship, we have a choice. We can keep things light and fluffy. We can be honest about the easy stuff but never the hard stuff. We can hide away the truth of who we are so no one will reject us.

Or we can be true to ourselves. We can take the risk of showing up all the way in our friendships. We can dive into the deep end and tell it like it is. We can **share** the things that are secret and hard and true and messy.

It's easy to stay in the safe zone—aka the fake zone—because of the what-ifs:

- What if they reject me when they really know me?
- What if they judge me?
- What if they don't love me anymore?

Friend, can I say **something** to you? If that happens, then those are not your **real** friends.

That's not what friendship is.

Friendship should be a safe space.

Friendship should be the place where we can erupt like a volcano, laugh like SpongeBob, and cry our ugliest without ever feeling judged. It should be a place for us to share what we're really thinking. It should be the place to be "too much." The place to be loud and hyper. The place to be tired and chill. The place to be quiet and just share space. The place where we make the most lopsided friendship bracelets and wear them with pride.

Sister, friendship is exactly where your mess belongs.

> Friendship should be a safe space.

MAKE YOUR OWN LIST!

Think of a friend you have who is different from you.
How are you different? Make a side-by-side list of
some of the ways you're not the same.

How do you feel about those differences? Do they bother you? Or do they make your friendship better? Explain why.

Notes for your Grown-Up

If you want to share your friendship journey with your grown-up, write some notes from this chapter here.

_____

_____

_____

_____

I have a friend named Erika who is really different from me. I love that we are so different. Here are just a few of the ways this shows up in our friendship:

She likes order. I'm more chaotic.

She eats organic, healthy food. I eat a lot of Chick-fil-A sandwiches.

She likes to dress in trendy clothes. I dress in casual clothes.

She doesn't like to take risks. I am random and a risk-taker.

She thinks before she talks. I talk before I think.

Her favorite day would be spent at the spa. My favorite day would probably be spent at the amusement park.

We're so different, but we're better together. We're real with each other. Our friendship is great because we don't have to pretend. We accept and love each other just the way we are.

I have always longed for sisterhood.

My deepest desire was to have friends that I could call my sisters. I wanted friends who would walk in my house and open the fridge. I wanted friends who knew me well enough to call me out when I was in the wrong. Friends who I could be real with. Friends who would be real with me. I wanted the I-know-what-she's-thinking-before-she-says-it kind of friendship. When I learned that the key to having that kind of sisterhood was showing up and being my real self, I found the friendships I'd been looking for.

It's really that simple. Finding friendships that are real is a two-step process:

Step 1: Get Real. If your conversations are stuck on homework or what TV show you're watching, maybe it's time to take a risk and drop a truth bomb just to see what happens. It could be anything. You could say that you had super sweaty

Take a risk and drop a truth bomb.

armpits before your last math test. Or that you're upset because you're outgrowing your favorite clothes. Or that you want to try joining basketball, but you're worried you'll be the worst at it. It could be anything. It just has to be real.

Step 2: Invite. Invite people to be real back. Ask questions that are deeper than "What's your favorite subject?" Ask what they like about their siblings and parents. Ask how they felt during the last school lockdown drill. If you know they've been having a hard time with something, gently ask about it. If they're sad, check on them. If they told you something big, ask if anything new has happened with that since the last time you talked.

If you're wanting something more than fake, something more than "I'm good, thanks. How are you?" then start with you. Every time you're real with others, you invite them to be real with you. So go out there, show up as you are, and say, "I'm real. And I'm not scared of your real if you want to share it."

STICKY NOTE CHALLENGE

Grab a sticky note and write, "Let's be real. I'll go first!" at the top. Below that, write something real that you haven't told your friend yet. At the bottom, write, "HBU?" Then share your note with your friend when you see her in class. Start a conversation about things that matter!

Did you find the secret message?

Write it out here:

8
When You're Feeling Left Out

I've lived in four different cities in Texas, and if I can tell you one thing about Texas, it's this—Texas is really, really big. So when I moved from Baytown to Lubbock, I knew no one. And I would have done anything to have a friend—one single friend. So I did the only thing I knew to do—I talked to people.

I looked for any reason to connect with other girls.

I'd go to coffee shops and scan the room for girls I had something in common with. "Oh, you're wearing a Taylor Swift shirt? 'Delicate' is one of my favorite songs. And look! I love this coffee shop too! Let's be besties."

I was always hoping that someone would notice me and talk to me. *Someone, anyone, please say hi to me. Tell me I have Dorito breath. I don't care. Just say something.*

I was seriously thinking about carrying a sign around with me that said, "Please just be my friend. I'll tell you you're pretty, and I'll let you pick the movie."

You know what the craziest part is? I would have made a great friend. I wouldn't have forgotten to text back or call. I wouldn't have forgotten birthdays or pets' names. And I had a lot of crazy stories, pee-your-pants-funny jokes, and extra sour gummy worms to give. I just didn't have anyone to share them with.

During this time, I learned all about loneliness. I learned all about being the only girl not invited to the party. I learned all about life on the outside of the circle.

But it taught me to stop looking inside the circle—or clique—for my people and to start looking for other outsiders like myself. When I looked around, I noticed that there were so many people outside the circle.

Rather than feeling left out every time I saw a social media post of a group of girls laughing together, I came up with a plan to change my situation.

First, I put myself out there. I tried some of the tips we talked about in chapter 2. Second, I asked my friends if they would be willing to introduce me to their friends. But the third thing I did was the most important. I looked for somebody else who needed a friend as badly as I did. Somebody who was new. Somebody who was often overlooked. Somebody who wasn't always included.

I'd been living in Lubbock for a few years at that point, and I had worked and worked to force my way in with a certain group. I'd invited them over. I'd reached out. I'd started conversations. I really thought I was part of the group. And then I found out there was a girls' night, and I hadn't been included. Now, I could have gotten over being left out once. That happens. But then I found out I'd been left out a lot. I realized that even though I believed these girls were my closest friends, they did not feel the same way about me. I was simply a nice girl they kind of knew. Turns out, I'd been trying to make friends the wrong way. I was trying to force my way into a group that didn't have **an open** spot.

I was still nice to them, of course, and they were still nice to me. I didn't stop liking them. They were really awesome people. They just weren't *my* people, so I stopped trying so hard and focused my attention and energy elsewhere. And then I remembered that the people who make the best friends are usually the ones

> The people who make the best friends are usually the ones who need a best friend.

who need a best friend. So I started thinking about everyone else who might have been an outsider too.

Callie came to mind. She was new in town, and I knew exactly how that felt.

Now, years later, Callie has become more like a sister to me than anyone else. I always keep a bag of her favorite pretzels at my house. We have matching french fry and hamburger sweatshirts, and neither of us cares how cheesy that is. I know her favorite drink at Starbucks. I help her with her cats. I even clean the litter box, which is so gross, but I do it with a smile because it's for Callie. (I'm more of a dog person because dogs are obviously the best, but that's okay.) We hang out on Friday nights eating pizza and playing board games just because.

Instead of forcing my way into the middle of a closed **circle**, also known as a clique, I found the answer to my prayers waiting on the outside all along. I just had to open my eyes, recognize it, and then be brave enough to break the ice.

So what's the difference between a clique and a friend group? How can you tell which is which when you're trying to find new friends? A clique is a small, closed-off circle of people who hang out only with each other and don't let others into their circle.

These are the signs that you might be dealing with a clique:

- Not all friends are equal; someone is the "leader."
- The group gossips or spreads rumors.
- The friends pressure one another to do certain things.
- The group tends to compete with one another.
- Group members make fun of people who aren't in their circle.[1]

A friend group, on the other hand, is a group of girls who share common interests, enjoy hanging out together, and encourage one another. These girls are happy to have new girls join in on the fun.

You can often tell that a group of girls is friendly based on their body language—the way they smile, stand, and look at you while you're talking to them.

If you're ready to ditch the cliques and make a fun friend group of your own, remember what it's like to be in these kinds of situations:

- Wondering if anybody really wants you there
- Not knowing anyone

BODY LANGUAGE
IS FOR Besties

DID YOU KNOW THAT THERE ARE LOTS OF WAYS TO TELL SOMEONE "I'M FRIENDLY" WITHOUT SAYING IT? THIS IS CALLED BODY LANGUAGE. HERE'S WHAT IT LOOKS LIKE:

Looking them in the eye
(BUT NOT THE WHOLE TIME)

Giving them your full Attention
(NOT LOOKING AT OTHER PEOPLE OR YOUR PHONE)

Being still
(NOT FIDGETING YOUR HANDS OR FEET)

making the same gestures as them
(FOR EXAMPLE, WAVE IF THEY WAVE)

Smiling after you notice someone

Turning your body toward them
(THINK SHOULDERS, NOT JUST YOUR HEAD)

uncrossing your arms OR legs

Keeping your feet pointed toward them [2]

- Standing around twiddling your thumbs, talking to yourself, and counting down the minutes until you can leave the lunch table or birthday party or backyard barbecue
- Not being included in a conversation
- Feeling like you don't belong in the circle

Then, don't forget to leave some space for new girls to be included in your circle. The goal is to shift your focus from trying to fit in with others to welcoming others—*not* to start a brand-new clique.

You're Welcoming

Scenario: You see a new kid sitting alone on the bus.
Action: Ask, "Hey, can I sit by you?"

Scenario: A girl transfers into your class.
Action: After class, ask, "Do you want to sit with me and my friends at lunch?"

Scenario: A new kid moves into your neighborhood.
Action: Ask, "Do you want to ride bikes or go for a walk so I can show you around?" (Don't forget to let your parents know!)

Scenario: You notice someone doesn't have a partner for a group project.

Action: Ask, "Would you like to join our group? We've got room for one more!"

Scenario: You notice a kid at the park or at a birthday party who isn't talking to anyone.

Action: Walk over to her and invite her into your conversation. You could say, "I was just telling this hilarious story that happened during school yesterday. You've got to hear it!"

Build your own space, look around, and gather up all the girls you notice hanging outside of the circle. You might just find some of your best friends there. And while it's great to find people who laugh at your jokes, maybe the most important ingredient in friendship is finding friends who want it as badly as you do. Friends who have room for friendship and room for you.

Here's the thing: we can't be best friends with everyone. In a perfect world, we'd be super close with every person we liked. We would share our secrets with them. We would talk to them all the time, and we would feel safe with them. But we don't live in that world. We live in a world where people have limits. Even you. You're crazy awesome, but you have to sleep sometimes. You only have twenty-four hours in a day, seven days in a week, and you've got things to do like school and homework and chores and sports practice and piano lessons. No matter how hard you try, you can't be best friends with everyone, and that doesn't make you a bad person. It simply makes you a person.

And don't forget, this works in reverse too. So the next time you're feeling the sting of being left out, remember this:

1. Everyone gets left out sometimes. You aren't the only one who has felt excluded.

2. If you get left out, it doesn't mean you aren't a wonderful friend and a great person.

3. Not everyone can be invited to everything. Sometimes people are only allowed to have one or two friends over, or sometimes they only invite the people from their classroom or gymnastics class. That's okay. I bet there have been times when you weren't able to invite everyone you wanted to a sleepover, a get-together, or a birthday party. And I bet it wasn't because you were trying to hurt the other person or because you didn't like them.

DROP SOME KNOWLEDGE!

Have you ever tried to be friends with a group
of girls but felt you were never really part of the
group? If yes, why did you feel that way?

_____

_____

_____

_____

_____

_____

_____

What did that teach you?

_____

_____

_____

_____

What is one thing you can do to make sure your
group of friends doesn't become a clique?

_____

_____

_____

_____

4. You've got a lot of other good things going in your life. Don't let the sadness or anger of one rejection hold you back. Forgive the other person and play it like Elsa: let it go!

5. You can have fun anyway! Make plans with somebody else. Ask your family if you can have a family game night. Have a dance party in the living room. Life is good. Enjoy it.

6. You'll have a chance to make sure someone else isn't left out in the future. Use it. The next time you're making an invite list, see if you can make room for one or two more. If you're inviting almost everyone from your class, group, or team, think about including everyone (as long as your grown-up says it's okay).

Stop trying to fit in and start inviting others in.

I didn't know it back then, but being left out was the best thing that ever happened to me. Why? Because I learned that I needed to stop trying to fit in and start inviting others in. I don't know where you'll find your people, but I know I found mine because I finally stopped trying to beg, force, and claw my way into the center of a circle, and I started looking on the outside.

Notes for your Grown-Up

Write down one or two things this chapter
made you think about that you'd like to
share with a grown-up in your life.

_____

_____

_____

_____

If you don't have a place to belong, try not to focus on how much that hurts. Forget about the invitations you didn't get or the group texts you were left off of or the birthday parties you weren't invited to. Instead, focus on building something better. Maybe they'll come. And maybe they won't. We have to accept that we have zero control over other people's actions. All we can do is be brave and keep trying.

It's scary and it's hard to try to make a group of your own. But know this: there is a very, very good chance that as you make space for and invite others into your life, you'll find the place where you belong.

STICKY NOTE CHALLENGE

Create your own mini-invitation on a
sticky note, and give it to a girl who
doesn't have a group of friends. Write
down the what, when, and where of your
hang-out idea, and then leave an option
to RSVP by circling yes or no. For example:

What: Movie night with Amy and Jess
When: Friday night at 6:30 P.M.
Where: My house
Want to come? Y/N

Did you find the secret message?

Write it out here:

__ __ __ __ __ __ __ __

__ __ __ __ __ __ __

__ __ __ __ __ __ __ __

9
When you're *Tired* of Competing

One time, my friend Elizabeth and I both decided to try out for the school play. I made it—Elizabeth didn't. And afterward, she wouldn't even talk to me. This went on for months.

To make matters worse, she convinced our other friend, Annie, not to talk to me either.

On opening night, all of the other cast members' friends were there to watch them and cheer them on. But mine weren't. I'd done a great job in the play, but it still felt like I'd fallen flat on my face.

There I was: unwanted, unliked, unincluded. It was yet another time when I felt like the girl standing there with her tray who didn't know where to sit in the cafeteria. The girl who wasn't "enough" to fit in. The girl who for some reason had to have more or be more or do more than other girls in order to belong. Or in this case, I guess I felt like I needed to be less.

But life isn't about being the most popular or the best dressed or the smartest kid in your class. Your worth does not come from the number of text messages you get in a day or the number of birthday-party invites you get from kids in your class. You are not more valuable when you get compliments on your outfit or get all As on your report card. It doesn't matter whether you hang out with friends every single weekend or you spend most Saturdays hanging out with your parents and your pet bulldog.

It's okay to strive for some of those things. It's okay if you have a goal to get all As this term or if you're practicing hard with the hopes of being the lead in your school play. It's okay to compete on the soccer field. Competition isn't bad when it's part of an activity. What's bad is when you make your life a competition.

So much of our time is spent trying to be the girl who has the most. The most friends, the most awards, the most trophies, the most activities, the most clothes, the most Valentine's Day cards. But all that does is lead to some harmful stuff like this:

- Creating drama
- Comparing yourself to others
- Feeling jealous
- Having self-doubt
- Pretending to be something you're not
- Pushing people down to get ahead

And (drumroll, please) *competing with others.*

We should be trying to level up our friendships, not trying to one-up our friends.

There should be no winners and losers among friends. We're all winners—and that is the goal. That's the whole point, the entire meaning of friendship: that we encourage **everyone** in the group. That we make sure everyone feels happy and loved and supported. That the people in our circle of friends make us feel better about ourselves—not worse. That we move from a mindset of "her versus me" and dive headfirst into a place of "we."

When a friend gets ahead, it doesn't mean you're behind. When she **wins**, it doesn't mean you lose. And when she comes in first, it doesn't mean you come in last.

> We should be trying to level up our friendships, not trying to one-up our friends.

We'll all get a chance to be in the spotlight; it just might be at different times. So we have to get comfortable with the idea that our friends are going to succeed and be praised on days when we aren't—and we can be excited for them anyway! After all, it won't be long until we have a win too. And, hopefully, they'll be excited for us in return.

Try to remind yourself that your time will come. Be grateful for all the good things **in** your life. Remember all the talents and skills you have and all the times you have been the one to get the spot, to win the game, or to have amazing things happen.

Let's celebrate each other. Celebrating is so much fun! I've learned that the second I feel even the slightest pang of jealousy is the time I need to turn my attitude around completely and do something nice for my friend. I give them a compliment, and I lift them higher. I write them a note and tell them how great I think they are. I buy them flowers. Or I dance and jump and scream right along with them and join in on **the** good time. Pouting is pretty miserable. I don't want to spend my life that way. I want to spend my life cheering instead.

We get to choose whether to be sunshine in our friends' lives or rain. Let's be sunshine and spread light and goodness so we can all grow.

Stop Your Stinkin' Thinkin'

INSTEAD OF	THINK
I want to be *the* best.	I want to be *my* best.
I'll *never* win.	I haven't won *yet*.
If she wins, I lose.	If she wins, that's great!
I need to have more.	I'm happy with what I have.
She's better than me.	We're good at different things.[1]

My friend Nikki was the best cheerleader ever. She didn't even have to work that hard at it. Her body would just flip around effortlessly. She was a natural at tumbling and jumping and doing stunts.

My body, however, didn't like to flip. It flopped like a sack of potatoes. I tried so hard to do flips like Nikki. I went to so many lessons and I worked at home like I was supposed to. But I couldn't bend and twist that way. At one football **game**, I accidentally did a roundoff right into the mascot, and we both ended up flat on our faces in a tangled heap—in front of the whole school. I was so embarrassed that I never tried to tumble again.

I'll admit, I was a little jealous of Nikki. I would have given my favorite pair of sneakers to be good at tumbling—maybe even my silver charm bracelet. But I am thankful that my jealousy never stopped Nikki and me from being friends. We went on to have many, many happy years hanging out.

It's normal to feel a little bummed when your friend gets the spot on the gymnastics team and you're left behind. It's normal to feel sad when your friend wins the volleyball game and you lose. It's normal to feel disappointed when amazing things keep happening to your friend and you're stuck in a rut.

What matters is what we do with those feelings. Do we let those feelings steal our joy? Do we let those feelings cause mean and hurtful things to come out of our mouths? Do we let those feelings come between us and our friend?

I sure hope not. Ugly feelings can quickly turn to ugly actions. And ugly actions can quickly turn to ugly relationships.

Feelings happen, and that's okay. The most important thing is that you tell your feelings to take a hike before you allow them to ruin a strong friendship and turn you into someone you don't ever want to be: a jealous green-eyed monster.

DON'T LET YOUR FEELINGS TURN YOU INTO A
Green-Eyed Monster

Don't let this ▶	disappointment when someone else gets something you want
Turn you into this ▶	a green-eyed monster who is angry at other people for what they have
Don't let this ▶	wishing you were as successful as someone else
Turn you into this ▶	a green-eyed monster who feels like a failure
Don't let this ▶	noticing someone else has a really nice wardrobe
Turn you into this ▶	a green-eyed monster who's trying to look cooler than everyone else
Don't let this ▶	wanting to be friends with someone you look up to
Turn you into this ▶	a green-eyed monster who tries to one-up her friends

As for me, I've realized that I am 100 percent in control of my feelings. I don't need to doubt myself or feel bad for myself. I may not always be the girl who leaves with a trophy or who flips the best, but I can be the girl who cheers the loudest, celebrates her friends the hardest, and has the most fun.

Their wins can become your wins too.

After all, when you don't see your friends as your competition, then their wins can become your wins too, and we can all celebrate together. What's better than that?

I never want to miss out on an opportunity to celebrate others in a major way because cheering for people gives me so much joy. It's fun to cheer for our friends and clap for our family. When we don't, we tend to get stuck in a "What about me?" pity party. And that's a party I *never* want an invitation to. There's never cake at a pity party, and I want to be where the cake is. More icing please!

So here are some things I've decided:

- I'll never let jealousy hold me back from a good time.
- I'll never let comparison and competition stand in the way of a good **friendship**.

- I'll never believe that there isn't plenty of room for each and every beautiful one of us to shine in our own unique ways.

So don't push other girls out; invite them in. Don't look at them as competition; look at them as inspiration.

Don't be fooled into thinking that tearing somebody else down could ever bring you higher. It will just end up tearing you down too.

We really can all win. We can all have our moment. We can do life better—as a team.

STICKY NOTE CHALLENGE

The next time you're feeling jealous, don't let that feeling turn you into a green-eyed monster. Instead, think about the ways you're proud of yourself. Then, grab a sticky note and write this to yourself: "Girl, I'm really proud of your _____." Or "Girl, I love your _____." Finish the note by writing, "I believe in you. I like you exactly the way you are." Then, stick that note next to your favorite spot in the house so you're reminded to be proud of yourself every day.

SLAY THE GREEN-EYED MONSTER!

Do you have a friend you often feel jealous of or feel like you need to compete with? Don't beat yourself up about this. It happens! But you can stop it from happening again. Make a list of at least three things you can start doing today to support your friend instead of trying to one-up her.

1. _____

_____

_____

_____

_____

2. _____

_____

_____

3. _____

_____

_____

_____

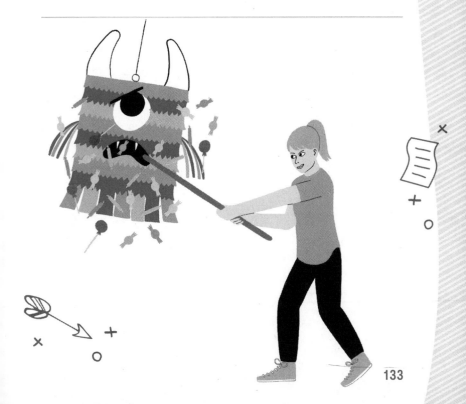

133

Notes for Your Grown-Up

Write down one or two things this chapter
made you think about that you'd like to
share with a grown-up in your life.

_____

_____

_____

_____

_____

_____

_____

_____

_____

_____

Stop sulking and go celebrate someone else. Start being the loudest cheerleader in the stands. These are your friends—not your enemies. You're not in competition with each other.

Support her. When you do, you'll both win.

Did you find the secret message?

Write it out here:

___ ___ ___ ___ ___ ___ ___ ___

___ ___ ___ ___ ___ ___ ___ ___

___ ___ ___ ___ ___ ___ ___ ___

10

When you're a Bad Friend

Confession time: sometimes I'm a bad friend.

I'm just guessing here, but I bet sometimes you are too.

It's important to be honest about that. I'm not saying to put yourself down about it. I'm saying, let's be honest about the fact that we mess up. That sometimes we're the problem. Let's be honest that even when we're doing our best, sometimes our best isn't quite good enough.

The truth is that if we're all trying to be perfect friends, then not a single one of us will succeed.

One time a friend wanted to borrow my favorite hoodie. I didn't know how to tell her no, but I was low-key obsessed with that hoodie and didn't want to lend it to her. She could borrow any other article of clothing I owned (even my favorite band tee)—just not that one.

I got stressed about saying no because I didn't want to hurt her feelings. But that backfired. The stress made me awkward, and I ended up blurting out, "No, sorry" *way* too intensely. Long story short, I did hurt her feelings. Not because I said **no** but because of how I said it.

I'm so glad she said something to me later so I could clear the air and let her know what was going on in my head.

Friendship is messy, and sometimes we're total jerkwads. I was a jerkwad in my fight with my hoodie-borrowing friend. I'll admit it. I had a bad attitude. Now we laugh about it because—well, everyone acts like a jerkwad sometimes.

Maybe you've had a bad-friend moment that looked something like this:

- Your friend asked you how you did on your math test. You didn't do so well, but instead of being honest about that, you said, "Why are you even asking?" and ignored her for the rest of the day. #badfriendmove
- You and your friend were playing video games, and she wanted to switch things up and go outside. You didn't. So you told her, "Well, you can just go home if you don't want to hang out anymore." #badfriendmove

- Some of your friends planned a sleepover. You were invited but weren't supposed to tell your other friend about it since she was left out. You went along with this plan because you didn't want to be left out too. #badfriendmove

- You and your best friend had a dumb argument. Instead of just agreeing to disagree, you dug in your heels and told her that her preference was stupid and she was wrong. #badfriendmove

- You got to go on a vacation to Disney World over spring break—a place your best friend has always wanted to go. When you returned, you bragged to your bestie about how great it was and didn't bother to ask about her spring break (after all, yours was cooler). #badfriendmove

The thing is, when you get close to another girl (like, really close), you also get up close and personal to each other's "real." That sounds all cutesy and nice on paper, but your "real" isn't just sharing your embarrassing stories and messy bedroom. Sometimes, "real" means making mistakes. Sometimes "real" is code for "yikes." When I wake up in the morning, my hair looks like I've been electrocuted. And my eyes are always a little puffy. It's not

GIRL, ADMIT IT!

We all act like jerkwads sometimes! Pobody's nerfect, am I right? So be honest and write about the last time you acted like a bad friend.

What happened?

_____

_____

_____

Why did it happen?

_____

_____

_____

How did you repair the friendship?

_____

_____

_____

How can you be a better friend in the future?

_____

_____

_____

_____

a good look. If that's how I start my day physically, you can imagine that I don't always wake up on the right side of the bed emotionally either.

The way forward is giving lots of grace to each other and promising to make things right when we mess up.

Don't give up just because you can't be **perfect**. When I was in school, my organization style was "keep shoving it in there until you can't shove anymore." My desk and locker got so full of papers, books, and things that smelled weird that I just stopped using it and started using my friend's instead. (Now that I think about it, I'm pretty sure she didn't love this.) Eventually, I realized that cleaning up was all or nothing for me. If I tidied my locker, it was *perfect*, **but** as soon as one single crumpled-up homework assignment got thrown in there, I gave up and didn't try at all.

I think it's easy to look at friendship in the same way: all or nothing. Amazing or nada. The perfect friend or "I just won't try." The problem is that being a perfect friend is too hard. We can't do it. We'll never be that.

Let me set the record straight: being a good friend does not mean being a perfect friend. It also doesn't mean any of these things:

> Being a good friend does not mean being a perfect friend.

- Always knowing the right thing to say or do
- Putting all your needs aside to make someone else happy
- Never feeling awkward or unsure
- Being available anytime, anywhere

Being a good friend means trying your best. It means showing up whenever you can. It means loving your friend smack-dab in the middle of the mess and chaos.

Being a good friend also means making mistakes. In fact, the closer your relationship, the more likely you are to screw up. When you're casual friends, you can mostly behave. You can pretend to be in a good mood when you're actually kind of cranky. You can smile and hide it when you're really having the worst day. But when you get really close to your friends, the crazy starts to leak through the cracks—like how my papers started poking out of my messy locker.

The good news is that one of the greatest gifts of friendship is to know your person and be known by them. There's not a single one of us who doesn't have flaws. There's not a single one of us who isn't going to screw up sometimes. But every single time you mess up and make it right, your friendship grows stronger.

Notes for Your Grown-Up

If you want to share your friendship journey with your grown-up, write some notes from this chapter here.

_____

_____

_____

_____

_____

_____

_____

_____

_____

_____

_____

We're going to keep showing up even when we make a big ol' stink with our bad attitudes. And we're going to say, "I'm sorry I was a total weirdo today. And I'm sorry I hurt your feelings."

The key is that when we make a mess, we have to show back up to the mess and clean it up, even if it's the hard thing to do.

I don't think we leave enough room for failure in our relationships. We need to stop talking about how not to fail and start talking about what to do *when* we do fail. So here are three steps we can take to clean up the messes we make.

STEP #1: STAY

Friendship isn't the place for "cancel culture." You can't be a good friend with a "one strike and you're out" mindset. *Hi, you can be my friend, but don't mess up, 'cause if you do, girl, bye.*

Our friends need to know that we're not going anywhere. We need to leave room to make mistakes. We need to leave room for failure (both theirs and ours). This isn't a performance, and it's not a test.

This is about belonging to each other in a way that's not easily breakable.

Sometimes, we "cancel" ourselves. Because we make a mess in our friendships, we feel like we need to pull away and move on. That can seem a lot easier than trying to clean up the mess we've made. But friendships are so precious, and they're not disposable. They're worth every single second we spend cleaning up after ourselves.

To be clear: I'm not talking about staying in a toxic relationship. I am talking about doing hard things for the sake of friendships that are worth it.

STEP #2: SAY YOU'RE SORRY

A few months back, I hurt a friend by accident. She was going through something really hard, and she felt like I wasn't there for her. Things felt weird between us, so I asked, "Hey, are we good?" She was brave enough to respond, "I don't know. I'm feeling hurt right now." We had an honest conversation, and I told her I was so sorry. I didn't mean to hurt my friend's feelings, but I had. So I owed it to her to listen and apologize.

When you make a mess, don't brush it under the carpet like a ten-thousand-pound elephant. Spoiler alert: it doesn't go away. To have close friendships, we need to make things right. Maybe it was an accident, or maybe you did something that was just plain ugly. Either way, don't pull away. Clean up your mess. Sit on the floor and listen. Hash it out. Say you're sorry.

STEP #3: SHAKE IT OFF (AIN'T NOBODY PERFECT)

Sister, you can't get everything right (and neither can anyone else).

We have to leave space for failure in our friendships. There has to be room for that, or the whole thing will come tumbling down like a tower of Jenga blocks. Shake it off. Dance it off. Do what you have to do, and let it go. Friendship is messy, and that's part of its beauty.

STICKY NOTE CHALLENGE

On a sticky note, write, "Friendships aren't disposable!" Then, stick it next to a trash can in your house. Every time you throw something away, remember that friendship messes are meant to be cleaned up—not thrown out. Be brave and try your best to make things right. Friendship is worth it.

Do You Owe Her an Apology?

Answer the questions below and follow the arrows to find out whether you owe your friend an apology. (Be sure to answer honestly!)

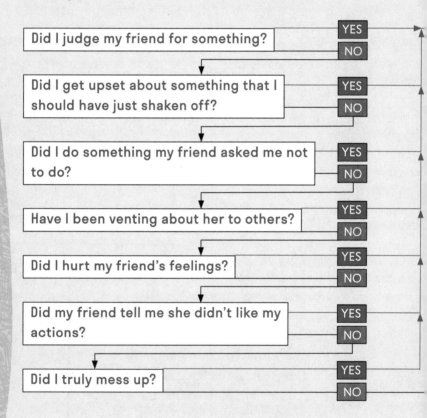

Did I judge my friend for something?
YES
NO

Did I get upset about something that I should have just shaken off?
YES
NO

Did I do something my friend asked me not to do?
YES
NO

Have I been venting about her to others?
YES
NO

Did I hurt my friend's feelings?
YES
NO

Did my friend tell me she didn't like my actions?
YES
NO

Did I truly mess up?
YES
NO

If you do owe her an apology . . .

Tell her you're sorry. Don't make excuses, and don't expect her to forgive you right away. Apologize because it's the right thing to do. Don't do it with the hope that it will suddenly fix everything. But after you say what you need to say, let it go. Don't beat yourself up about it. Just spend some time thinking about how you can do better in the future. What mistakes did you make? What have you learned? Again, this isn't about criticizing yourself or feeling guilty. This is about making sure you become the great friend you want to be.

If you don't owe her an apology . . .

If you decide an apology is not in order, this also might mean the friendship has reached a breaking point. If that's the case, that's okay. Remind yourself that friendship breakups happen (more on that in the next chapter!). They are a part of life. Remember the relationship for what it was, and remind yourself of all the future friendships waiting for you. I genuinely believe that every broken friendship gets us one piece closer to the right friendship.

149

PERFECTLY YOU

NOBODY IS PERFECT—AND THAT'S OKAY! WHEN WE CHOOSE TO LOVE OURSELVES AND OUR FRIENDS EVEN THOUGH WE MAKE MISTAKES, WE BECOME MORE OF THE FOLLOWING:

CREATIVE · forgiving · COURAGEOUS

PERSISTENT · UNDERSTANDING · COMPASSIONATE

THOUGHTFUL · MOTIVATED

THESE ARE MUCH BETTER QUALITIES TO AIM FOR THAN

"PERFECT."

IN THE SPACE BELOW, WRITE A SHORT LETTER TO YOURSELF ABOUT WHY YOU LOVE AND ACCEPT YOURSELF JUST THE WAY YOU ARE.

You make mistakes. So what? Me too. Mistakes paired with forgiveness belong in friendships. Ask for forgiveness from your friends, but don't forget to forgive yourself. Leave your mistakes in the past where they belong. Keep moving. Shake it off.

Sometimes we are the bad friend. But just because we weren't perfect doesn't mean we can't make things right and move forward. The next time you mess up, remember the three S's:

1. Stay
2. Say you're sorry
3. Shake it off

Then, do what you can to be a better friend next time. I believe in you.

Did you find the secret message?

Write it out here:

_ _ _ _ _ _ _ _ _ _ _ _ _ _ _ _ ,

_ _ ,

_ _ _ _ _ _ _ _ .

11
When You've Had a Friend Breakup

I don't know why I'm writing this chapter.

I've never been through a friend breakup.

And yes, thank you for asking, it is really hard being so popular.

I'm kidding.

I have friends—I actually have *amazing* friends—but I only have like one friend I hang out with all the time. I plan a girls' night every couple of months—nothing crazy. And sadly, I've definitely been through my fair share of friend **breakups**.

Friendships break. It **happen**s. They rip and shift, and they lose their strength from time to time. They end, and they leave you hurt and confused.

What happened?

What could I have done differently?

How could someone treat me that way?

I know we want everyone good in our lives to stay in our lives. **But** sometimes, things change. And we don't have any control over it.

Sometimes even the most solid of friendships crumple like a piece of notebook paper. Sometimes there isn't a reason. But sometimes there is. Maybe you've experienced **some** of these reasons:

- Moving somewhere far away
- Saying hurtful things to each other
- Breaking each other's trust
- Not listening to each other
- Refusing to understand each other
- Realizing the relationship isn't healthy
- Realizing you just don't have enough in common

For every million breakups, there are a million different reasons why.

There's also one reason that's becoming more and more of a problem: social media.

Whatever the reason, I don't know anyone who hasn't been hurt by a relationship gone wrong. For a long time, I

WE COMMUNICATE BETTER

IF YOUR FRIEND DOESN'T UNDERSTAND YOU, TRY SAYING IT AGAIN! IF YOU WANT TO BE SURE YOU UNDERSTAND HER, ASK FOR CLARIFICATION. YOU MIGHT SAY, "IT SOUNDS LIKE YOU'RE SAYING _____ . IS THAT RIGHT? OR AM I CONFUSED?"

WE CAN READ BODY LANGUAGE

LOOK BACK AT THE CHART "BODY LANGUAGE IS FOR BESTIES" ON PAGE 114. IS YOUR FRIEND COMMUNICATING THAT SHE'S FEELING OPEN AND FRIENDLY? OR IS SHE FROWNING, LOOKING AWAY FROM YOU, FIDGETING, AND SITTING WITH HER ARMS CROSSED?

Let's "FACE" IT

GETTING TOGETHER AND TALKING IN PERSON OFTEN LEADS TO BETTER COMMUNICATION THAN WHEN WE TRY TO HASH THINGS OUT IN A TEXT OR CHAT—OR EVEN A VIDEO CALL. WHY? BECAUSE WHEN WE TALK FACE-TO-FACE . . .

WE PICK UP ON NONVERBAL CUES

NOTICE YOUR FRIEND'S TONE OF VOICE AND FACIAL EXPRESSION. WHAT DO THEY TELL YOU? FOR EXAMPLE, MAYBE HER EYEBROWS ARE SCRUNCHED TOGETHER, WHICH TELLS YOU SHE MIGHT BE FEELING UPSET OR CONFUSED. MAYBE HER EYES ARE WIDE, WHICH TELLS YOU SHE'S SURPRISED. MAYBE HER LIPS ARE PRESSED TOGETHER IN A STRAIGHT LINE, WHICH TELLS YOU SHE'S ANNOYED. OR MAYBE HER CHEEKS ARE RED WITH EMBARRASSMENT.

WE LISTEN MORE THOUGHTFULLY

MAKE EYE CONTACT AND LISTEN TO YOUR FRIEND—WITHOUT ANY DISTRACTIONS.

WE CAN OFFER COMFORT

IF YOUR FRIEND IS OKAY WITH IT, GIVE HER A HUG. PHYSICAL CONNECTION CAN MAKE FORGIVENESS EASIER.[1]

thought I was the only one who had ever had this kind of painful experience.

But I've since realized that I'm not the only one who has lost a friend. Not by a long shot. And neither are you. Friend breakups are simply a part of every girl's life. But here's the good news: even when one friendship ends, there's always hope that another amazing friendship will come along in the future.

Another amazing friendship will come along.

I've learned a lot from my friend breakups—about both myself and others. I've also learned what to do and what not to do when confronted with the possibility of a friend breakup. And I've learned about what to do to get to the other side. Here are five things I've learned that I'd like to share with you:

1. **Let yourself feel sad.** For whatever reason, I think people try to pretend that everything is fine after a friend breakup. Maybe it's because we're embarrassed about how the friendship ended. Or maybe we think it's silly to be upset about it. But we have no reason to hide our feelings. It's okay to be sad.

SELF-CARE TIPS

It's okay to feel sad when you're going through a friend breakup. It's normal. But if you're having a hard time getting past it, these tips can help you deal with those hurt feelings and replace them with hope for the future.

Take belly breaths

Breathe in through your nose and fill your belly up with air. Then exhale through your mouth and let it all go.[2]

Go for a walk

Move your body to release feel-good hormones and look around at nature to give yourself a sense of peace.[3]

Color

Use crayons, markers, colored pencils, paint, or anything else you want. Release your emotions onto the page.[4]

Stretch

Stretch your body to help your mind relax. Try lying on your back and grabbing your feet in the air. This is called the "happy baby" pose.[5]

It's okay if it takes a while to get over a friendship. Breakups hurt. But they hurt less when you're honest about your sad feelings and are able to share them with others.

2. **Don't be bitter, and don't shame or blame.** It's okay if you're sad or mad after a friend breakup. But you don't have a right to hate your former friend or gossip about her. Just because a friendship ends does not mean it has to cause drama, and it does not mean you have to be enemies. It's so tempting to blame the other girl and treat her like the villain. But there's always another side to the story, and there's almost always something we could have done differently. Blaming keeps us from understanding others. And it keeps us from understanding our own mistakes. And it keeps us from understanding how to make relationships work better in the future. Playing the blame game doesn't benefit anyone—not her and not you.

3. **Learn the things you need to learn.** There's always something to learn from a friend breakup:

- Maybe you learn about yourself—like learning that you prefer to make solid plans instead of just "going with the flow."

- Maybe you learn about the things you do well—like communicating when you've had a bad day.
- Maybe you learn about the areas where you need to improve—like listening or keeping your emotions under control.
- Maybe you learn about boundaries—like telling your friends that you sometimes need alone time to recharge.
- Maybe you learn how to let things go—like when you and your friend disagree about something silly.

I don't know exactly what you'll learn, but you'll learn something. Hopefully, it will help make your next friendship stronger.

4. **Start fresh.** One of the worst things you can do in a new friendship is expect it to be like your **last** one. Don't assume that this friendship will end the same way the other friendship ended. Don't assume that this friend will laugh at the same things your other friend laughed at. Don't assume that a game your other friend didn't like is off-limits in this friendship. Don't assume anything. This isn't the same

Notes for your Grown-up

If you want to share your friendship journey with your grown-up, write some notes from this chapter here.

_____

_____

_____

_____

_____

friendship, and this isn't the same person. Give it a chance. Start fresh. Ask lots of questions about what they like and what they don't like. Discover all the new things you might enjoy doing together.

5. **Let it go and see what happens.** I'm all for loving people. I am not, however, into begging, bugging, manipulating, guilting, or clinging. If someone needs space and wants to walk away from the friendship, please let them. If they tell you

they don't want to hang out, don't try to convince them otherwise. If they stop responding to your texts, don't send them passive-aggressive texts to show them you're hurt. If they go off and try to make different friends, don't try to force your way into that new group. You can be disappointed that they're no longer spending time with you. But don't be desperate. Let it go and see what happens. Once in a while, friendships circle around like a boomerang. Sometimes life brings you two back together. Suddenly, you're in the same homeroom again partnering up on a group project, and things click back in place. Sometimes the weirdness from before makes the relationship even stronger. If the relationship was mostly good—if there is something to be saved—don't be afraid to reconnect. You never know what the future holds.

Every friendship has a season. Whether that season is your whole life or maybe just for the school year, try to appreciate each friendship while you have it. I can't promise you that you won't lose some of those friends someday. But I can promise that even if you do, you can still have hope for the future.

GET SOME CLOSURE!

Part of what makes a friend breakup so difficult to move past is that it's sometimes hard to know why things ended. We're left hurt, confused, and scratching our heads. But even though it takes two people to build a friendship, you can get closure all on your own. Here are two ways:

1. Journal. Write about the good times and the things you learned through the breakup.

The things I loved about my friend:

_____

_____

162

The things I did well in this friendship:

_____

_____

The things she did well in this friendship:

_____

_____

How some things could have been better:

_____

_____

Why I am proud of myself:

_____

_____

Some things I will be looking for in my next friendship:

_____

_____

2. If you're ready, write a letter of forgiveness to your former friend. This is for your eyes only (it isn't something you're ever going to send). Make it as honest and real as you need. The point is to give you a chance to think about your feelings and then let them go. Sometimes it helps to put the truth down on paper rather than just think it in our heads. I'll go first.

Dear _____,

What you did wasn't okay, and forgiving you doesn't say that it was. You really hurt my feelings. But I forgive you.

I know I didn't do everything perfectly either. I made mistakes. But I forgive me too.

I'm not going to carry this around anymore. I'm letting it go.

Amy

Now it's your turn! On a separate piece of paper, write a letter to your former friend.

Once you've written your letter, give yourself a minute to reflect on what you wrote, then trash it. Cut it into itty-bitty pieces. Make it into a wad and

shoot a two-pointer into the wastebasket. That friendship is in your past, and throwing away your letter shows that you're ready to forgive and move past it. Now the only thing in front of you is a future full of hope.

I get that it's scary to try to make friends when there are no guarantees that your friendship will last. I wish that wasn't the case. I wish I could have been the one to figure out the magical formula for making friendships last **forever**. Mostly because that would be helpful. But also because I'd be *rich*. (Rich enough to buy that little farm I've always wanted—with my sheep, Ed Sheepran and Lady BaaaBaaa; my cow, Dairy Styles; my chickens, Hendaya and Hennifer Lopez; and Arillama Grande, who is obviously a llama. Okay, okay. I'm done.)

STICKY NOTE CHALLENGE

Grab a sticky note and write, "I forgive her, and I forgive me—and I'm open to future friendships." Then stick it on the back side of your bedroom door. Every time you close the door, read the note and remember to close the door on old wounds and past friendships. Every time you open the door, remember that there are still many other friendships out there—just waiting for you.

(And my donkey, Snoop Donk. But for real now, I'll stop.)

Even if there are no guarantees, friendship is always worth the effort of putting yourself out there. Whatever happened in the past, there is always hope for the future.

> Friendship is always worth the effort of putting yourself out there.

Did you find the secret message?

Write it out here:

___ ___ ___ ___ ___ ___ ___ ___ ___

___ ___ ___ ___ ___ ___ ___

___ ___ ___ ___ ___ ___

12

when your Words matter

Words matter; use them for good.

When I was in second grade, my bangs started halfway back on my head and were an inch thick. It was clear that my mom cut my hair at home.

The day Mom decided to let me grow them out was very exciting for me, mostly because my forehead hadn't felt a cool breeze in years.

Little did I know that growing out bangs is not for the faint of heart. It takes a long time, and the not-quite-grown-out bangs is not a cute look.

Over the following months, my mom plastered my bangs to my head every morning with so much gel that it looked like I'd just taken a shower. Every day they stayed put until one o'clock, when the gel wore off just in time for

PE. Halfway through my first lap around the gym, I could feel them loosen, and then *thwap*—a giant chunk of hair would smack me in the forehead.

With each step, the bang clump would bounce back on my head and then, *thwap*, hit me on the forehead again. It was like my bangs were waving at my friends. *Bounce, bounce, thwap, thwap.* It probably lives on in the whole class's memory. (*"Do you remember how Jessica Cushman's hair used to wave at us during dodgeball?"*)

One morning my archenemy, Libby, who got chocolate bars in her lunch and took credit for my art projects, sneered at me from across the table with her Elmer's glue bottle in hand. "Is this what's in **your** hair?" she asked. "Why is your hair so greasy? Is it glue? It's like beeswax." I ignored her and continued cutting up my shapes. "Beeeeeeeswax, beeeeeeswax," she sang.

I do not remember a whole lot about second grade except the bang flapping and the beeswax.

It's crazy how **words** stick with us, isn't it?

You may think this chapter isn't for you. After all, you're super nice! But let me ask you this—have you ever done one of these things:

• Whispered a rumor you heard about someone?

YOUR WORDS HAVE POWER

- Called someone a mean name on the internet?
- Talked about a friend behind her back?
- Told everyone except your friend why you were mad at her?

Sister, I'm guilty of it too. It's a whole lot easier to focus on other people's flaws than deal with my own. It's a whole lot easier to talk smack about someone than to have a conversation with them to work things out.

Words are hard. They're also powerful. We **can** use our words to build each other up or tear others down.

Don't believe me? Then believe science.

Back in 2018, an IKEA store conducted an experiment to discover the impact of words on plants.[1] For thirty days, two plants received equal light, nutrition, and water inside their individual enclosures. They also received messages through speakers. But the messages were different: one plant was being bullied, and the other was being told encouraging things. After thirty days, the plant that received compliments and encouragement was healthy and thriving. The plant that was insulted and bullied was drooping and wilted. Isn't that amazing?

> We can use our words to build each other up.

What's your Communication Style?

When I'm chatting with my friends, I like to . . .

a) Think before I speak—and listen a lot

b) Tell jokes—the more laughs I can get, the better!

c) Lead the conversation by asking lots of questions

d) Only talk about things everyone understands so no one feels left out

My favorite form of communicating is . . .

a) Sending texts or chat messages

b) Sending GIFs or emojis

c) Emailing or writing notes

d) Talking in person

When I'm talking to others, I usually feel . . .

a) A little nervous—I don't want to say the wrong thing

b) Energized and bubbly—I love talking

c) Cool and confident—I know it will be a good conversation

d) Calm and attentive—I don't want to miss anything

When I'm talking to someone, it bugs me when they . . .

a) Don't take a moment to let me respond to their questions
b) Don't laugh at anything I say—are they made of stone?
c) Have a conversation with only one person instead of paying attention to everyone
d) Talk over me and other people

When I meet someone new, I usually . . .

a) Talk about school or something else basic—we don't know each other well yet
b) Tell a joke—or three—to break the ice
c) Share everything about me—I'm an open book
d) Ask lots of questions to get to know them better

IF YOU GOT MOSTLY A'S:

You're a thinker. You often let others do the talking. But that doesn't mean you don't have a lot to say! You just like to think on it first so you don't say something you'll regret later.

IF YOU GOT MOSTLY B'S:

You're a socializer. You like to be the center of attention. And you're happy to tell jokes and stories to get the party going! You're good at brushing things off with a laugh.

IF YOU GOT MOSTLY C'S:

You're a commander. You're organized and like to keep conversations on track. You're probably the one to suggest a game of truth or dare—and make sure everyone plays by the rules!

IF YOU GOT MOSTLY D'S:

You're a connector. You're super thoughtful and great at making other people feel comfortable. No one will be left out on your watch![2]

STICKY NOTE CHALLENGE

Grab a sticky note and write something on it that will make your friend smile! Give her a compliment or some encouragement—it doesn't have to be long. Then, the next time you hang out at her place, stick it somewhere in her bedroom where she will find it later and feel encouraged by your words.

As it turns out, words literally hold the power of death and life.

If a plant without emotions or a soul thrives with encouragement, how much more do we?

There's a girl in my life who can be "a lot." But I adore her. So even when she's being a little extra, I let her know I love who she is. I tell her she's my favorite kind of spicy. Because we always have a choice: we can either **point out** the gold in each other or go mining for garbage. I want to be someone who chooses gold.

Every single person will say things we don't agree with and do things we think are annoying. Every. Single. One. We have **the** choice to focus on that or to focus on the beautiful things that make them *them*.

Let's be people who use our words to make others feel good about themselves, not tear them down.

One of the best ways we can practice using our words for good is to be honest and direct. You can rant on and on about how awful it is that so-and-so did such and such. But unless you are honest with that person about what they did to upset you, nothing will change. In fact, it will only get worse because now you'll be adding hurtful words to an already painful situation.

One of the best communication tools I've learned in my friendships is to resolve conflict quickly by being honest in the moment. It could be as simple as saying, "Hey, what did you mean when you said that? It seemed like you meant this, and it hurt my feelings" or "Sometimes when you do that, I feel like you don't like me very much." Most of the time when I've tried this, my friends were surprised. They had no idea I felt that way, and they were quick to make it right.

Sometimes the thing we have to tell our friends isn't that our feelings are hurt—it's that their behavior is a little off. For example, one time a friend nicely called me out for being defensive. Basically, I was acting like everyone was out to get me when, **in** reality, no one was out to get me. This happened during a group hangout. I didn't say anything mean to anyone, but I had a weird attitude because I was so concerned about everyone having a good time.

It was a super-hot summer day, and I was worried the girls who came over to my house wouldn't be comfortable because my family didn't have any air-conditioning. I made sure all the windows were closed and turned the fans on. I also got everyone water.

That's when my friend Aubree innocently said, "Whoa, it's hot out today."

I immediately got defensive. "Hot? I don't think it's hot. The fans are on. It's nice and cool."

"Okay," she said.

Later, after most of the other girls had gone home, she brought that conversation back up to me.

"Hey, why did it bother you so much when I said that it was hot earlier?" she asked.

"What? It didn't bother me," I said.

"Are you sure? Because it really seemed like it did."

When I realized she was right, we were able to laugh about it. But I'm so glad she chose to talk to me. She could have rolled her eyes and vented to another friend about how I was being weird and defensive. She could have let herself grow more and more frustrated every time I showed that same quirk (because I wouldn't have realized I was doing it unless she said something). But she didn't. She just asked me about it.

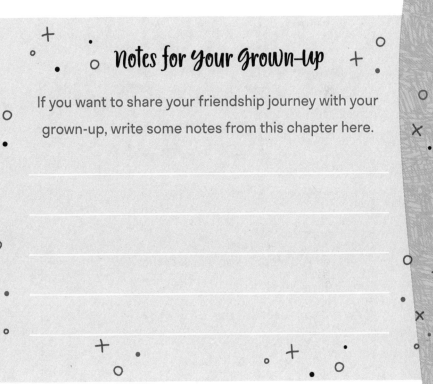

Notes for your Grown-up

If you want to share your friendship journey with your grown-up, write some notes from this chapter here.

If we don't ask the hard questions, and if we don't speak to our friends directly and honestly, how will we grow? If we don't call one another out once in a while, how will we ever recognize our blind spots? How will we ever get better at friendship?

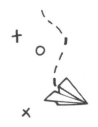

THIS IS YOUR SPACE TO BE CREATIVE! COLOR, JOURNAL, AND DOODLE ALL YOUR THOUGHTS.

USE YOUR WORDS FOR GOOD!

Let's start practicing healthy communication. We can ask questions:

- "What did you mean when you said that?"
- "Hey, are we good?"
- "Why did you react like that?"
- "Did I hurt your feelings?"

We can tell each other how we feel:

- "Hey, when you did that, it hurt my feelings."
- "Can we talk about the other day? I felt like things got weird between us."
- "I've been struggling with _____. Can we talk about it?"
- "When you do _____, I feel _____."

We can listen well and apologize sincerely:

- "I was really grumpy today, and I took it out on you. I'm so sorry."
- "Hey, after I said that, I realized it was really insensitive. Will you forgive me?"
- "I'm sorry I'm being kind of weird today. I'm not feeling good."
- "You're right. I'm so sorry I did that."

Communication is a powerful tool. When we ask questions, share how we feel, listen well, and apologize, it takes our friendships to a whole new level.

Now it's time for you to practice! Think about the last time you wanted to share something hard with a friend, but you didn't. Maybe it's too late to go back and say it now, but it's not too late to learn from that experience and practice how you'll respond in the future. Write down what you would say about it today. Reread the lists above for inspiration.

_____

_____

_____

I don't know about you, but I value the honest friends I have in my life. Although it might hurt in the moment, having people around me who will tell the truth is so valuable.

If we have a friend who has hurt us (and we value them), we need to use our words for good and talk to them. We don't need to talk to our other friend who has nothing to do with it. That's a form of gossip. It might feel good to vent, but it's not going to get us any closer to the friend we have the issue with. It's also not going to get us closer to the friend we're venting to.

We have to stop the gossip.

We have to stop the gossip and be honest with our friends instead.

Remember how I said words are powerful? They are. That's why gossip is so damaging—not just to the people being gossiped about but also to the person doing the gossiping. Friendships formed by bonding over gossip never last long because you can't trust each other. We have to learn to stop the name-calling and story-spreading.

I've been the gossiper, and I've been the girl who was gossiped about. The first is slimy, and the second is painful. Gossip only leads to broken hearts and broken friendships.

So let's put a stop to it.

Use Your Words To...

Find and circle all the words hidden in the grid below.
Remember to look in every direction!

WOW
BOOST
CHEER

ENCOURAGE
DREAM
EXCITE

ASK
SHARE

V	Q	G	A	F	E	N	N	S	C	L	D	C	K	U
A	A	B	G	T	V	K	T	F	K	V	L	Q	O	C
T	S	S	L	T	G	Z	O	W	W	G	V	G	Z	Z
D	Q	Q	K	S	P	T	D	S	N	A	U	S	Y	G
M	G	A	J	H	M	G	Q	H	N	U	B	F	U	U
R	A	E	N	C	O	U	R	A	G	E	O	B	J	I
E	R	X	P	S	U	X	T	R	A	F	O	I	C	M
T	G	H	F	S	F	H	E	E	L	K	S	E	G	B
V	Z	W	C	Z	X	F	G	A	P	D	T	M	H	N
D	U	P	Q	O	D	O	H	Y	Q	I	V	P	C	W
S	K	S	H	P	Y	C	T	J	C	P	Z	R	L	V
V	I	G	J	U	C	H	O	X	S	D	Z	H	W	N
U	G	H	R	V	M	E	E	R	R	E	W	O	W	C
Z	U	T	Y	D	R	E	A	M	G	W	N	O	L	C
V	O	F	L	R	Q	R	F	Y	J	Z	W	F	O	Q

What if, instead, we stood up for other girls? What if we spent our energy cheering them on instead of criticizing them? What if we went out of our way to build our sisters up?

It's so easy to be against one another. It's easy to assume the worst about **others**, to tear others down, to blame, and to find fault. But it doesn't have to be that way.

We get to choose. We get to choose the kind of sisterhood we want.

Let's resolve conflict bravely, and let's stop gossip when it comes our way.

Let's use our words for good.

Did you find the secret message?

Write it out here:

___ __ ___ ___ ____ __ __

__ ___ ___ ___ ____ ___ __ _

__ _ ___ ___ __.

Conclusion

Well, this is it. You now have all the tools you need to make and keep real-life friendships!

Just the fact that you read this book says a lot. It says:

1. You want good friendships.
2. You're willing to give and do hard things to make those friendships work.
3. You're willing to learn.

And these three things are what you need most on your journey to making great friends.

Please remember, you are not alone on the journey. We experienced awkward arguments on the playground in elementary school. We walked our middle school hallways without knowing where we belonged. We remember. And even though we're all grown up (with our daughters now on those playgrounds and in those hallways), we're with you. We're in this friendship thing together.

Being a good friend isn't something you're born with. It's something you learn. And, goodness, we wish we would have had a book like this to help us get there.

From the time we were little, all the adults in our lives asked us what we wanted to be when we grew up. I (Jess) wanted to be a garbage truck driver at age four, an animal rescuer at age ten, and a zoologist at age twelve. Spoiler: I didn't become any of those things. In the end, I'm not sure "What do you want to be when you grow up?" is that important of a question.

You know what is an important question? "What kind of friends do you want around you? What kind of friend do you want to be?" We wish somebody had asked us that.

It's kind of like going on a trip. Yeah, it matters where you're headed, but it matters more who's along for the ride (and that you packed a good snack).

The question "What do you want to be?" is all about you—and that's important. But we also need to think about us and we. Whatever your goal is for the future, you're going to want friends in your life while you get there. You're going to want them when everything is sunshine and ice cream and when everything is stormy and there's a bad lunch in the cafeteria.

There may be different friends in different seasons, but learning what you need in a friend and how to be a good friend will help you develop deep sisterhood in every stage of life.

Friendship is so, so important at every single age.

We crave closeness with people more than we crave FLAMIN' HOT CHEETOS and sour gummies (and I don't know about you, but we're obsessed with those). It's the way we're wired. No one ever promised that doing life with others would always mean holding hands and skipping along. No one ever said we wouldn't sometimes get our feelings hurt. But even in all our messes and mistakes, there's something inside us created to help one another, to carry one another, and to love one another.

So, if you're looking for somewhere to start, look for someone who needs a friend.

We don't know where you're at right now. Maybe you have a ton of close friends. Maybe you've recently lost the friends you thought you'd always have. Maybe you just moved. Maybe your family is going through something, and it's been hard and lonely. Maybe you don't know if you have anyone you can call a true friend.

No matter where you're at right now, no matter what your friendships have looked like in the past, no matter how many people you know (or don't know), hear this: there is hope, and you're not alone.

You can do this.

It won't be perfect.

It won't always work the way you want.

Every once in a while, it will probably turn out like that one time you tried tie-dyeing T-shirts and everything (including your hands) turned a disgusting shade of poop brown.

But remember, there are a million girls behind you on this journey, there are a million right where you are, and there are women (like us) who are ahead of you, showing you the way. We're woven together like the colorful threads of the most beautiful friendship bracelet. And each friend is like a string in that bracelet. We bring our own unique gifts, personalities, and talents to the table, and each one is special and made with a distinct purpose. That's the magic of it: we are good on our own, but we are so much stronger when we all come together.

WORD SEARCHES

A GOOD FRIEND IS . . .

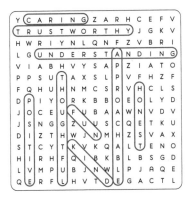

A GOOD FRIEND MAKES YOU FEEL . . .

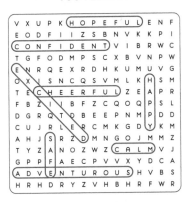

REAL FRIENDSHIPS ARE . . .

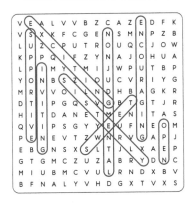

USE YOUR WORDS TO . . .

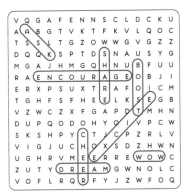

SECRET MESSAGES

Chapter 1

You can do this!

Chapter 2

Someone great is waiting
to be your friend.

Chapter 3

Friendship takes time.

Chapter 4

You are a friend
worth having.

Chapter 5

We can ditch the lies
and find the truth
about friendship.

Chapter 6

You are amazing
just as you are.

Chapter 7

Take a chance and share
something real today.

Chapter 8

An open circle is better
than a closed circle.

Chapter 9

Everyone wins in the
game of friendship.

Chapter 10

Nobody is perfect, but
you're still pretty great.

Chapter 11

Breakups happen, but some
friendships last forever.

Chapter 12

Your words can point
out the gold in others.

notes

Chapter 1: When You Really Need a Friend (Yeah, Us Too)

1. Carl Zimmer, "Friends with Benefits," *TIME*, February 20, 2012, http://content.time.com/time/subscriber/article /0,33009,2106488,00.html; Ohio State University, "Like College Roommates, Vampire Bats Bond When Randomly Paired," ScienceDaily, April 6, 2022, https://www.sciencedaily .com/releases/2022/04/220406101740.htm; Christa Lesté-Lasserre, "Killer Whales Form Killer Friendships, New Drone Footage Suggests," *Science*, June 17, 2021, https://www.science .org/content/article/killer-whales-form-killer-friendships -new-drone-footage-suggests.

Chapter 2: When You're Lonely

1. "Cigna 2018 U.S. Loneliness Index," Cigna, accessed June 10, 2022, https://www.cigna.com/assets/docs/newsroom /loneliness-survey-2018-updated-fact-sheet.pdf; Nayanah Siva, "Loneliness in Children and Young People in the UK," *The Lancet Child & Adolescent Health* 4, no. 8 (August 2020): 567–68, https://doi.org/10.1016/S2352-4642(20)30213-3; "Is Your Child Lonely? (For Parents)," Mental Health America, accessed April 3, 2022, https://mhanational.org/your-child -lonely-parents.

Chapter 3: When It Takes Time to Level Up Your Friendships

1. Michael P. McManmon, *Autism and Learning Differences: An Active Learning Teaching Toolkit* (London: Jessica Kingsley Publishers, 2015), 300–301; "Dunbar's Number: Why We Can Only Maintain 150 Relationships," BBC Future, 2019,

https://www.bbc.com/future/article/20191001-dunbars
-number-why-we-can-only-maintain-150-relationships;
Maya Riser-Kositsky, "Education Statistics: Facts About
American Schools," Education Week, updated January 7, 2022,
https://www.edweek.org/leadership/education-statistics
-facts-about-american-schools/2019/01; Jeffrey A. Hall, "How
Many Hours Does It Take to Make a Friend?," *Journal of Social
and Personal Relationships* 36, no. 4 (April 2019): 1278–96,
https://doi.org/10.1177/0265407518761225.

Chapter 4: When You Don't Feel Confident

1. KidsHealth Medical Experts, "Confidence," Nemours
TeensHealth, accessed May 19, 2022, https://kidshealth.org
/en/teens/confidence.html#catbest-self; Emmaline Soken-
Huberty, "10 Reasons Why Confidence Is Important," TIS!,
accessed May 19, 2022, https://theimportantsite.com
/10-reasons-why-confidence-is-important/.

2. Mayo Clinic Staff, "Teens and Social Media Use: What's the
Impact?," Mayo Clinic, February 26, 2022, https://www
.mayoclinic.org/healthy-lifestyle/tween-and-teen-health
/in-depth/teens-and-social-media-use/art-20474437;
Lawrence Robinson and Melinda Smith, "Social Media
and Mental Health," HelpGuide, updated October 2021,
https://www.helpguide.org/articles/mental-health/social
-media-and-mental-health.htm; Ben Stegner, "7 Negative
Effects of Social Media on People and Users," MUO, updated
December 27, 2021, https://www.makeuseof.com/tag
/negative-effects-social-media/; "Effects of Social Media
on Children," Cleveland Clinic, December 3, 2021, https://
health.clevelandclinic.org/dangers-of-social-media-for
-youth/; Nicole Fabian-Weber, "8 Dangers of Social Media
to Discuss with Kids and Teens," Care.com, March 2, 2021,
https://www.care.com/c/5-dangers-of-social-media-to
-discuss-with-you/; Abby Moore and Kristina Hallett,

"12 Ways Social Media Affects Relationships, From Research & Experts," September 21, 2020, MBG Relationships, https://www.mindbodygreen.com/articles/social-media-and-relationships.

Chapter 5: When You're Pretty Sure You've Been Tricked

1. "Bystanders Are Essential to Bullying Prevention and Intervention," StopBullying.gov, May 21, 2021, https://www.stopbullying.gov/resources/research-resources/bystanders-are-essential; "Statistics and Laws," Riverside Medical Clinic Charitable Foundation, accessed May 19, 2022, https://www.rmccharity.org/bullying-prevention-institute/resources/facts-and-laws/; School Jotter, "Stop Bullying! Infographic," eLearning Infographics, November 6, 2015, https://elearninginfographics.com/stop-bullying-infographic/; "Bullying Facts & Statistics," Our Kids Are Why, accessed May 19, 2022, https://www.whyinc.org/bullying-facts-statistics; "Bullying Statistics," Family Resources Furtherance Project, accessed June 11, 2022, https://www.frfp.ca/bullying-statistics/; "11 Facts About Cyberbullying," DoSomething.org, accessed May 19, 2022, https://www.dosomething.org/us/facts/11-facts-about-cyber-bullying.
2. Valerie Ross, "6 Scientific Reasons Why Your Friends Really Do Make You Happier," Birchbox, accessed May 19, 2022, https://www.birchbox.com/magazine/article/6-scientific-reasons-why-your-friends-really-do-make-you-happier.

Chapter 6: When Someone Doesn't Like You

1. Devrupa Rakshit, "Why People-Pleasing Is a Common Human Instinct," The Swaddle, November 6, 2020, https://theswaddle.com/why-people-pleasing-is-a-common-human-instinct/; Robert F. Kushner and Seung W. Choi, "Prevalence of Unhealthy Lifestyle Patterns Among

Overweight and Obese Adults," *Obesity* 18, no. 6 (June 2010): 1160–67, https://onlinelibrary.wiley.com/doi/pdf/10.1038/oby .2009.376; Sherri Gordon, "How People Pleasing Contributes to Bullying and How to Stop It," Verywell Family, updated June 5, 2021, https://www.verywellfamily.com/people -pleasing-contributes-bullying-460646.

2. Lisa Natcharian, "Real Learning: Meet the Perfectionists," MassLive, July 15, 2010, https://www.masslive.com/real _learning/2010/07/meet_the_perfectionists.html; Jessica Grose, "How to Help Your Perfectionist Kid," *The New York Times*, July 1, 2020, https://www.nytimes.com/2020/07/01 /parenting/perfectionist-kids.html.

3. Kelsey Torgerson Dunn, "Why Your Teen Automatically Thinks the Worst," Compassionate Counseling St. Louis, May 28, 2018, https://www.compassionatecounselingstl .com/blog/why-our-kids-automatically-think-the-worst; "Data and Statistics on Children's Mental Health," Centers for Disease Control and Prevention, March 4, 2022, https:// www.cdc.gov/childrensmentalhealth/data.html.

4. Sherri Gordon, "Pros and Cons of Competition Among Kids and Teens," Verywell Family, updated September 17, 2020, https://www.verywellfamily.com/competition-among -kids-pros-and-cons-4177958; Katie Hurley, "How Toxic Competition Is Ruining Our Kids—And What to Do About It," *U.S. News & World Report*, March 8, 2018, https://health .usnews.com/wellness/for-parents/articles/2018-03-08 /how-toxic-competition-is-ruining-our-kids-and-what-to -do-about-it.

5. American Girl, "Friendship Style Quiz," 2015, http://www .americangirlpublishing.com/wp-content/uploads/2015/07 /Printable-Activities-Truly-Me-Friendship-Quiz.pdf; Stellaciarapica13, "Answer This Quiz with 100% Honest and We'll Reveal What You're Actually Like As a Friend,"

BuzzFeed, April 26, 2021, https://www.buzzfeed.com
/stellaciarapica13/what-kind-of-friend-are-you-3jp9nboa29.

Chapter 7: When Everyone Seems Fake

1. SaraBeautyCorner, "DIY Friendship Bracelets. 5 Easy DIY
   Bracelet Projects!," September 14, 2014, on YouTube, video,
   6:30, https://youtu.be/YujvDp5BJ78.

Chapter 8: When You're Feeling Left Out

1. Karin Lehnardt, "44 Exclusive Facts About Cliques," Fact
   Retriever, August 22, 2017, https://www.factretriever.com
   /clique-facts; Rosalind Wiseman, Queen Bees and Wannabes
   (New York: Three Rivers Press, 2009); Sherri Gordon, "How
   to Tell the Difference Between a Clique and Friends,"
   Verywell Family, updated March 29, 2022, https://www
   .verywellfamily.com/a-clique-or-friends-how-to-tell-the
   -difference-460637; Kathryn Hoffses, "Coping with Cliques,"
   Nemours TeensHealth, July 2018, https://kidshealth.org/en
   /teens/cliques.html; Alison Clarke-Stewart and Ross D.
   Parke, Social Development, 2nd ed. (Hoboken, NJ: John Wiley
   & Sons, Inc., 2011), 257.
2. Toria Sheffield, "Ways to Be Your Best Self Through Body
   Language," Bustle, June 10, 2016, https://www.bustle.com
   /articles/166064–9-body-language-tips-that-make-people
   -want-to-be-around-you-more.

Chapter 9: When You're Tired of Competing

1. Julianna Cario, "How to Help Children Stop Comparing
   Themselves to Others," Big Life Journal, August 6, 2021,
   https://biglifejournal.com/blogs/blog/how-to-help-children
   -stop-comparing-themselves-to-others.

Chapter 10: When You're a Bad Friend

1. Alexandra Eidens, "7 Ways to Help Your Kids See the Beauty of Imperfection," Azoomee, accessed June 11, 2022, https://www.azoomee.com/blog/7-ways-to-help-your-kids-see -the-beauty-of-imperfection; Karen Young, "Anxiety in Children—10 Practical Strategies to Help Kids Manage Perfectionism," Hey Sigmund, May 2018, https://www .heysigmund.com/anxiety-in-children-10-practical -strategies-to-help-kids-manage-perfectionism/.

Chapter 11: When You've Had a Friend Breakup

1. Maggie Wooll, "Why Face-to-Face Communication Matters (Even with Remote Work)," BetterUp, January 11, 2022, https://www.betterup.com/blog/face-to-face-communication; "5 Benefits of Face-to-Face Communication," Value Prop, June 25, 2021, https://www.valueprop.com/blog/5-benefits -face-face-communication; Laura Vanderkam, "The Science of When You Need In-Person Communication," Fast Company, September 30, 2015, https://www.fastcompany.com/3051518 /the-science-of-when-you-need-in-person-communication.

2. Kayla Craig, "11 Simple Self-Care Habits for Kids," PBS, December 15, 2020, https://www.pbs.org/parents/thrive /simple-self-care-habits-for-kids.

3. Bright Horizons Education Team, "Benefits of Nature for Kids," Bright Horizons, May 15, 2020, https://www .brighthorizons.com/family-resources/children-and-nature.

4. Lisa Currie, "11 Impressive Benefits of Mindful Coloring Pages for Kids and Adults," Ripple Kindness Project, accessed May 21, 2022, https://ripplekindness.org/benefits -of-mindfulness-coloring-for-children-and-adults/.

5. Sanjana Lagudu and Dr. Sandeep Jassal, "15 Best Yoga Poses for Kids," Mom Junction, May 9, 2022, https://www .momjunction.com/articles/easy-and-effective-yoga-poses -for-your-kids_00377906/.

Chapter 12: When Your Words Matter

1. "Bully a Plant: Say No to Bullying," video shared by IKEA UAE, April 30, 2018, on YouTube, https://www.youtube.com /watch?v=Yx6UgfQreYY.

2. "What's Your Communication Style?," Personality Lingo, accessed May 21, 2022, https://personalitylingo.com /free-communication-style-quiz/; Nayomi Chibana, "The 4 Communication Styles: Which One Do You Have? [Quiz]," Visme, September 16, 2015, https://visme.co/blog/the-4 -communication-styles-quiz/.

about the authors

Amy Weatherly is a Texas girl through and through, which is where she lives with her husband, three kids, and two rescue dogs—Lou and Brewster. She is passionate about helping women embrace courage, confidence, and purpose for their lives, and she does it with a quick wit and down-to-earth sense of humor. She has written for the *Today Show*, MSN.com, *Good Morning America*, Yahoo.com, and Love What Matters.

Jess Johnston lives in Southern California with her husband and four kids, who are the loves of her life. Her favorite thing to do is to sit around a table with her best friends, eating nachos and laughing until her stomach hurts. She has been a top contributor to publications such as *HuffPost*, *Scary Mommy*, and *Motherly*, and has been honored with *Motherly's* Writer of the Year Award.

YOU ARE Brave. YOU CAN Do this.